POSTSCRIPT FROM HIROSHIMA

Rafael Steinberg

POSTSCRIPT FROM HIROSHIMA

RANDOM HOUSE
NEW YORK

For my mother and father

POSTSCRIPT FROM HIROSHIMA

1°

As starkly familiar as a persistent nightmare, the backdrop is known to all mankind. The bright, cloudless sky, the clocks at 8:15, the three silver planes high overhead, and the work battalions in the streets, unconcerned because the all-clear had sounded. And then the nightmare begins.

First came the *pika*—the flash—and a hundred thousand people perished. Then came the blast—and the city was gone. Then came the mushroom cloud, and the living dead crying for water, and the rubbery faces sloughing off like masks, and the corpses awash in the seven-fingered delta of the Ota River.

Afterward, came peace.

Peace for the scarred survivors—to whom the dreadful dream is real and vivid memory—a peace uneasy with the fear of hidden ills and latent death.

Peace, with a chance to build a new, and better, and more prosperous city.

Peace for the stark shadowgraphs, etching on stone and pavement the last human instant of another age.

Peace for the dead to rest in, and "Peace!" for the living to chant.

The shadows are fading in Hiroshima today, and the visible scars are few. On the Yorozuyo Bridge, where the heat flash roasted nine pedestrians and imprinted their clear white shadows in the roadway, the surface has been repaved.

The owners have repainted the water tower a mile and a quarter from the Bomb; for years it bore the fixed shadow of a steel spiral staircase, as if the sun had halted in a bright sky.

A man, name unknown, who was sitting in front of the Sumitomo Bank, perhaps waiting for it to open, absorbed the flash and left his shadow on the granite wall and stone steps when the Atom Bomb exploded three hundred yards away. That shadow is fuzzy now, and dim, under the plaque that marks a "memento of the Atomic Bomb Explosion," and it no longer holds the shape of a man, but it is still there if you look closely, though hardly anyone does.

There are not enough sharp shadows left, in fact, for the scientists who still want to use them to calculate the exact location and altitude of the explosion.

Living shadows, where a shoulder strap protected the flesh beneath, or where the white pattern on a cotton dress reflected heat rays that the dark portions of material absorbed, leaving walking checkerboards, or where an upraised hand shielded part of a face— these may remain, but they are kept hidden. For these victims of the Atom Bomb, and for those whose scars lie within, World War II has not yet ended. Hiroshima is bigger and more prosperous than before, and within it is a new generation of young adults who do not remember or care; and to symbolize recovery, Japanese officials chose a Hiroshima Prefecture boy born three hours after the *pika* to carry the Olympic torch into the stadium in 1964—but the casualty lists in Hiroshima and Nagasaki have never been closed, for the victims of A-Bomb radiation are still dying there, before their time.

"But the bitterness is gone," a civic leader tells American visitors. "You will not find hatred. No one will throw rocks at you because you are American."

At dusk, in the Park of Peace, lovers approach to lie in the summer grass; under the willows weeping down to the river bank, solemn schoolchildren snap shut their paint boxes and tenderly roll up their pictures of the cenotaph, the monument to the dead. In the river, gay red and blue rowboats glide across the green water, propelled, it seems, by bursts of youthful laughter, while above them, silent, thoughtful fishermen lean over the railing of the Aioi Bridge, content and at peace.

But it is on this bridge that the cross-hairs of the *Enola Gay*'s bombsight were locked, that hot, sunny morning more than twenty years ago. And there beside it, the grim unrepaired ruin of Hiroshima's industrial exhibition hall looms over the bobbing rowboats like a stage set for tragedy. Piles of masonry lie tumbled in the weeds behind the remaining walls, and on top, like a crown of thorns, the rusting steel skeleton of the building's blasted dome is etched in black in the gathering mist. There was the hub of the holocaust, almost directly above the dome, and without thinking, the visitor glances up, searching. The Peace Bell in the park tolls with a hollow, throbbing sound. The shadows deepen. A soft breeze rustles the garlands of folded paper cranes draped on the Children's Monument. If there are ghosts, I am thinking, now is the time for them to speak.

A hand touches my elbow, and a smiling high school boy is standing there, speaking awkward English. "May I have conversation with you, sir?" He

6

clutches a phonograph record in its cellophane and cardboard sleeve. "You are American?"

Yes.

"This record. You know?"

No.

"You know Beatles?" the boy asks. I nod. "They are very good. Very good music. You know New York?"

Yes, I know New York.

His face shows delight. "You know *Cash Box* magazine? *Billboard* magazine?"

I suppose I do, but . . .

"Do you know, how can I get?"

Why do you want to get *Billboard* magazine?

"I want learn American songs. American jazz, very good, very good. Please, how can I get?"

His name is Toshio Nishiura, and he is seventeen, and he comes often to the Park of Peace to practice his high school English on foreign visitors, and his favorite record, the day I spoke to him, was "Mr. Lonely," sung by Bobby Vinton. Toshio's mother was in Hiroshima when the Bomb dropped, presumably received a dose of radiation, and worried, like all Hiroshima parents, about whether her children would be affected. But Toshio seems to have all the normal instincts of his generation: among other things, he longs to visit America some day. For him, the Atomic Dome, as the ugly, rusty ruin of the exhibition hall is called, is merely part of the permanent furniture of his town, like cannons in the parks of small-town America, and he is barely aware of it.

But for the scarred, the sick, the bereaved, the Dome is a public symbol of private suffering. Left as it stood to commemorate the disaster, and now the focal point of the monuments in the Park of Peace, the Dome is the last great visible scar on the face of the city, and the survivors seem to regard it as a license to remember.

Mrs. Aiko Hamada remembers frequently—every time the Hiroshima Carps play a game at home. The city's new baseball stadium stands right across the street from the Dome, and Mrs. Hamada, who is forty-five and a little stooped, has to pass right by the ruin on the way to her job in the concessionaire's booth under the grandstand, just along the third-base line. She rents out seat cushions and sells buns and candy to season-ticket holders, and earns $1.40 a day, or "more if it's a double-header." Although the Carps spend most of their time in the Central League cellar, Mrs. Hamada cheers them loyally and relentlessly, even when they are playing out of town and she has to watch on television.

Mrs. Hamada is a vivacious and emphatic talker in the rolling accent of western Japan, and her tale spins out so neatly, apparently unencumbered by emotion, that in the first few minutes after I started talking to her, it all seemed too unreal and unnatural to be true. And then it became clear that the smooth narrative, the chuckles, the expressive gestures and the exaggerated inflections were a form of psychological closure, and that only by speaking of the events as though they were a movie she had seen could she speak of them at all, or bear to remember.

"I was pregnant then, but I didn't know it yet. Just about a month, probably. My oldest girl was staying with my mother, in Niho. That's over behind Hijiyama, so they were protected. And my husband, he had come back wounded from the war, was down in Ujina on some veteran business." With twenty-six other housewives from her neighborhood association, Mrs. Hamada had been put to work on one of the many labor teams that were demolishing buildings to make firebreaks for the incendiary raids which Hiroshima, unscathed up to that moment, was expecting soon.

"I saw the plane, circling, it seemed, and it dropped something white that I thought was some more of those propaganda leaflets." The Bomb, at that moment, was already falling; what Mrs. Hamada, and thousands of others, saw was a parachute carrying a monitoring device dropped from a plane behind the *Enola Gay*. "I had been a little late, and I had just taken a drink of water from a faucet that remained from one of the houses we had torn down, and I must have been in the shade of a wall or a house, because when I saw the bright flash, and I dropped to the ground, terrified, a pile of tiles and wood and dirt and dust fell on top of me and I thought to myself, 'I'm going to perish here, like this.' "

But she didn't perish, although twenty-three of the twenty-seven housewives did. Mrs. Hamada thought herself lucky—until her boy was born the following March. "He didn't even live a few hours. He was underdeveloped, and the cord was all rotten, and we couldn't even bathe him. His skin was all loose, hanging kind of funny, and my husband says it was just like the skin of those people he had seen right after the *pika*, loose skin falling off like a torn shirt . . . But I think now, if I had not been pregnant, I would have died like the others in my group, or I would

10

have A-Bomb sickness now, like so many others. We don't know, of course, but I think he took the poison from me. I think that baby saved my life."

Mrs. Hamada is tough, and before that baby came she had already faced death, and walked through "First Street, Hell," as she and other survivors call it now, and she had seen the corpses stretched out on the street, stomachs bloated, waiting for the mass graves. She had breathed the stench of rotting flesh, and watched her friends cry pitifully for water she could not give them, and watched them die. But she is tough, and she bore two more children.

Her eldest daughter, born before the Bomb, is now twenty-two, and works in the offices of the Osaka Ginza Golf Trading Company. The two youngest, also girls, are in high school. In their tiny four-room rented house, the theme song, smack-smack, of "77 Sunset Strip" blares from the TV, competing with the jazz on the stereo set in the other corner. Kayoko Hamada, seventeen, is choosing the records and shaking her hips to the beat. She is long-limbed for a Japanese, and lithe, and saucy by nature. She plays volleyball for her high school team, stands a charming head taller than her mother, wears a shingle bob and likes to prance around the neighborhood of an evening in tight pink pants. Occasionally, Kayoko and her friends sally forth to the Peace Park, "just to fool around." She grins as she says this, and the tip of her tongue pokes out of the corner of her lips as if she were pretending to bite it off, and she tosses a sidelong glance at her mother, and giggles as she looks back at me.

"Are you studying English in school?" I ask her.

"I hate English."

"Why?"

"I'm Japanese, that's why."

So Japanese is Kayoko that she sees five or six American movies every month, and prefers the Beatles to all other musical possibilities. She cannot recall learning anything about the Bomb in school, and sums up her life with a bored shrug: "No matter what we do, there's nothing to get excited about."

Her mother sighs and shakes her head. It is "to give the kids some education and culture" that Mrs. Hamada works in the ball park, for her husband's salary as a minor civil servant doesn't quite cover living expenses and high school fees as well. (Free schooling goes only through junior high school.) But she really doesn't understand what is happening. "Young people nowadays are educated like Americans. They have ideas that are completely different, and they do things that pain our eyes to look at."

But the Atomic Dome doesn't bother her eyes. "People who did not see the *pika* do not understand. They say the Dome is ugly, but I see it every day and I don't think it is so ugly that it should not be kept as a reminder that such a tragedy should not be permitted to happen again. It is said that with the wind whistling around it all these years, and the rain beating on it, it may soon fall down by itself. Well, if it does, I will be sorry to lose it, but it can't be helped. But it would not be right to pull it down on purpose, as so many people are suggesting."

The Atomic Dome glowers over the river at the Park of Peace from the north. Facing it across the park at the southern end stands the world's grimmest collection of the relics of war—the Peace Memorial Museum. Here are the scorched tiles, and the fused coins, and the twisted bottles, and the huge photographs of victims grotesquely scarred. Here are the wax dummies, with department-store mannequin faces and gruesomely realistic wounds, draped with scorched and tattered clothing found in the ruins. Here is a steel girder bent by the force of the blast, a bicycle twisted into a tangled snarl, tools melted, pottery stuck together, a shattered clock stopped at 8:16, bones. For the scientifically minded, charts and maps explain the workings of the Bomb and the degrees of devastation in various parts of the city. For

13

the sentimental, there is the diary kept by a young girl who died of leukemia several years ago and subsequently became the heroine of a propaganda movie; the diary even includes daily notations, in the girl's own hand, of her worsening blood count.

Nowhere in the museum, or in the tape-recorded description which visitors can hear in Japanese or English by renting a receiver and earphone for twenty-eight cents, is there any mention of the United States government's contention that the Bomb saved lives in the long run because it brought the war to a quick end. The closest thing to it is one ambiguous sentence in the Japanese version of the recording: "When the Pacific war was finally about to end, at the stage where only a decisive battle on the mainland remained, the sudden disastrous event of Hiroshima was truly unfortunate to the people of Hiroshima, Japan and the whole world." There is no hint that the Bomb in fact ended the war, and the net effect that museum visitors take away with them is that of an unexplained and wanton barbaric act. "It was," says the English version, "the most tragic sight men had ever known in this world."

Some American visitors are affronted by the omission, and emerge fuming. "Do they want everyone to think we did it just for spite?" asked one tourist

14

from California. "It's disgraceful, much more shocking than any of those gruesome exhibits." Others, however, walk silently down the stairs into the sunlight of the Peace Park, numbed by what they have seen. One of these, an elderly lady, barely whispered: "I didn't realize until now how lucky we are that we had the Bomb and not them."

The director of the museum, Sukeharu Morihiro, is proud of the fact that an average of two thousand people, nearly half of them schoolchildren on organized tours, pass through the exhibits every day. He looks pained when asked why no explanation of the war is given; the possibility of false impressions doesn't bother him. Everyone knows about the war, he feels, and the museum is not the place to justify America. Any explanation would be bound to dissatisfy somebody, so the matter is just omitted, and controversy averted. The Japanese are not likely to be pleased to hear that 200,000 civilians were killed in Hiroshima in order to spare the lives of a like number of American soldiers; such a decision is one that any warring government might make, but even though most Japanese admit their leaders would have used the Bomb if they had one, the explanation is not one that would win friends for the United States. Logic also perished in the blast.

15

"Numerous people, maybe two or three hundred thousand, lost their lives or were injured." So states the flat American voice on the museum earphone device. It sounds like wild exaggeration to visitors who have done their homework and know that the "official" figure of Hiroshima dead, or at least the official American figure, is 78,150 and that only 61,443 names are inscribed within the granite block of the cenotaph. But it is one measure of the Hiroshima disaster that not even today can anyone state with any assurance of accuracy how many scores of thousands of people died under the Bomb. The Japanese version of the audio guide puts it simply: "The number of dead and missing could not be counted."

They have been counted, by inference and by analysis, over and over again, and the weight of the evidence suggests, unfortunately, that the vague upper figure lies closer to the truth that will never be known. One reason for the uncertainty is that the Occupation authorities took out of Japan all military records, including documents that could have shown how many soldiers were present that morning at the Imperial Army's Second Corps Headquarters almost directly under the explosion. They also took away certain civic records, such as ration card registers, that would give a more precise estimate than is available of the number of people living in the city on August 6th.

The official figures originated in a report made in November, 1945, by the prefectural police, who emphasized that their reckoning did not include military personnel. Strangely, their estimate differentiated between 78,150 dead and 13,985 missing, although only a small fraction of the victims were identified before their hurried burial in mass graves, so even by the police figures, more than 90,000 civilians in Hiroshima were killed. Furthermore, when the police made their count, Bomb victims were still dying as a direct result of the *pika*.

If the police estimate had been accurate, Hiroshima Mayor Shinzo Hamai points out, the number of dead, including military, would still have been well over 100,000. But Mayor Hamai, who was a city official at the time, says that the police deliberately underestimated the casualties, to please the Occupation forces as well as to avoid alarming the populace, who had enough to worry about in that first postwar winter.

"We really don't know how many died," the mayor admits. "We've investigated in many ways but no reliable total has been worked out. In the monument are the names only of those of whom we are sure, but on the basis of the number of people who must have been in the city, the total of dead comes out to about two hundred thousand." The official population of the city at the time was about 400,000, but many women and children and some factories with their workers had been dispersed to rural areas for safety. At the time of the Bomb, according to Hamai, there were actually about 250,000 residents of Hiroshima. To that, Hamai adds: 30,000 soldiers, which would have been a minimum; 70,000 workers from the country who had come in to help the city demolition crews; and 20,000 people from all over Hiroshima Prefecture who would flow into the prefectural capital for business, shopping or work on an average wartime weekday.

The total comes to 370,000. In 1950 a question on the national census poll elicited the information that 158,607 Japanese then living had been in Hiroshima on August 6, 1945. Which means, if the mayor's estimates are approximately correct, that 200,000 persons died under the Bomb or soon thereafter.

Numbers may mean people, but people are not numbers. Yet the mayor, after twenty years of it, discussed the terrible figures as if, as a historian, he had been musing on the deaths of faraway tribes in an ancient plague, not talking about his own town and life and experience. It is the only way he *can* discuss it, of course, because he is the one who adds a few hundred more names to the list of known dead under the granite block of the cenotaph every August 6th, and he must confront the issue and struggle with its legacy of problems every day of his life. The event was too cataclysmic for normal emotions to be set loose on it; the survivors must continue to survive, and to flourish.

Life, and laughter too, flourish on the macabre grounds of the Park of Peace. Signs along the paths admonish citizens that the park is a "place of repose," but they come to romp with the kids, polish their cars, do push-ups, make pickups, hold rallies, give speeches, sing in chorus, and pounce on stray foreigners to practice their English. A new bronze bell is intended to be struck as a prayer for peace, but gangs of teen-agers swing in delight on the big wooden clapper, vying with each other to see who can produce the loudest sound, like farm boys ringing the bell with a mallet at a country fair. Hoodlums find the park a good hunting ground, and city officials recently had to install a public phone in the park for the express purpose of enabling citizens to call the police in a hurry when the peace of the Park of Peace is broken. Even in the museum itself, the

touring bands of gawking, chattering students shuf-
fling through in tennis shoes make serious reflection
nearly impossible.

This carnival atmosphere appalls sensitive foreigners who approach Hiroshima with graveyard steps,
prepared to mourn. "I was shocked to find beer signs
in the park, and all that noise and ice cream," said
a thoughtful and intelligent matron from Madison,
Wisconsin. "It seemed to me like a Fourth of July
picnic, where people go to have a ball. I have a guilty
conscience about Hiroshima, as all Americans do,
and this shocked me. Maybe you shouldn't expect
people to walk through it like a cemetery, but it is
a cemetery, after all . . . And then I gave it second
thoughts. Why not? It's only healthy human nature
that people come here to relax on their day off. Perhaps it's a good sign that children can enjoy themselves again in Hiroshima."

In the center of this pleasure field, carved in a
flowing Japanese script on the granite face of the
cenotaph, the motto of Hiroshima greets those who
come to pray. "Rest peacefully, for the error shall
not be repeated." It is a curiously potent phrase.
Most Americans, upon having it translated, assume
that "error" refers to the Bomb, and go away abashed
or truculent, according to their prejudices. But it was

Japanese who objected when the stone was first un-veiled; one mother even insisted angrily that her young child's name be removed from the monument because he had not been guilty of any error.

The literature professor who composed the phrase is dead, but a friend of his insists that "he always said it meant the error of mankind, not the error of one side or the other." Wherever the *ayamachi*—the error—lies, the hope that it shall not be repeated is voiced over and over again in Hiroshima. It is shared by the rest of the world too, of course, but somehow it seems to mean more from the lips of people who know exactly what they are talking about.

Stand at the cenotaph with the *hibak'sha*—"the people who received the Bomb"; listen to the mur-mur of their prayers, and the tolling of the Peace Bell, and the laughter of children on the lawns around the monument, and gaze over the block and through the arch to the Atomic Dome. The Dome is crumb-ling, they say, and dangerous to passers-by, and it takes up valuable real estate that could contribute to the economic development of the city; some peo-ple want to tear it down, others want the city to spend money to preserve it.

For two decades this symbol of destruction ruled

the skyline of the city, a living scar in ragged silhouette, a numbing shock for the visitor and an ever-present reminder of tragedy for *hibak'sha* like Mrs. Hamada. But in 1965 a nine-story office building of steel and concrete rose behind it, dominating it, belittling it, making it nearly invisible from some directions. Now it is the blue-gray slate façade of the Chamber of Commerce and Industry Building that visitors view, with the Dome, through the cenotaph arch, and the old ruin begins to resemble part of a slum-clearance project that the wreckers have just started on.

Many *hibak'sha* resent the fact that a private commercial structure was permitted to "make the Dome look bad." It is painful that the Dome appears just shabby now, instead of tragic, because to them the ruin is not only a scar, but is a survivor like the living *hibak'sha;* it is the only recognizable public relic of the old Hiroshima. "Half the visitors say the new building profanes the sacred ground," reported the *Asahi Shimbun,* Japan's leading newspaper. Mayor Hamai thinks it makes the background of the park "look sort of queer." But, he points out, "we have no authority to forbid the construction of such a building on private property, and Hiroshima has developed so quickly lately that it could not be helped."

If the Dome testifies to the power of the Atom, the handsome new building behind it speaks even more eloquently of rebirth and reconstruction, and the power of human perseverance.

2°

Come to Hiroshima's Hondori to see the progress and prosperity of Japan. Hondori means Main Street, and it was widened after the Bomb; but other streets around it have been broadened even more in the new city plan, and carry more traffic and have sidewalks, and Hondori looks like a side-street arcade in comparison. But it is still the place to shop or stroll. Vehicles are banned from Hondori in daylight hours, and it is jammed with pedestrians and bicycles, and the stores are overflowing with appliances and stylish clothing and candies and books. Walk through here, and stop and talk awhile to the shopkeepers.

To enter the big furniture house of Morikichi Sera, customers have to squeeze through narrow aisles between rows of towering cabinets and wardrobes made of the ugly dark brown wood that is fashion-

24

able in Japan because it is so un-Japanese. In a back room, the exuberant, crew-cut proprietor is squatting on a cushion before a low lacquer table, for a cup of green tea and an hour or so of chat. Beside him, eyes round behind thick spectacles, sits his thirty-five year-old son and heir, Kikuo, lethargic and respectful. They are solid citizens, conservative, affluent and very lucky, having survived the Bomb without serious illness or injury in the family.

The elder Sera and his wife were spared because with no business to do at the drag end of the war, they had moved out to the family's suburban villa. Son Kikuo was saved because he was a slow poke: all the other boys in his class and on his demolition crew had already taken off their shirts in the hot morning sun, and many died of flash wounds. Kikuo's shirt was still on his back when the Bomb burst 1,100 meters away, so his burns were mild and he recovered quickly. A sister just happened to be in the shadow of a wall when the *pika* exploded.

With property on the Hondori, and in a trade that would soon profit from the westernization of Japanese living patterns, Sera was able to reopen for business in 1947 and recoup in a short time. Chuckling now, he recalls how he helped his luck along. "There was a law at first, that no building covering an area more than fifteen *tsubo* [about twenty-three by twenty-three feet] could be constructed. Well, I had enough property, so I built three buildings of fifteen *tsubo* each—and then later I knocked the walls down between them and had a store . . . That's the way we had to do things in those days."

Today, with thirty-six employees, with a new and even larger store and wide reputation, Sera is far more prosperous than before the war and has become a vice-president of the Chamber of Commerce and Industry. As might be expected, he is outraged by the suggestion that the Chamber's new building is a sacrilege.

"That's just nonsense. If they want to talk about sacred ground, then all of Hiroshima is sacred, because people died everywhere in the *pika*, not just around the Dome. It's all right to call it a memorial, but there's nothing sacred about that bit of land. If it had just been a local paper, or a Communist sheet that had said that, well, so what? But for a national paper like that—it's shocking. Actually, there's something else behind it." Some of Sera's colleagues in the Chamber point out that Hiroshima, like other Japanese cities, already has a surplus of office space; they think that some of the owners of other buildings might have inspired the criticism in order to keep their tenants from moving into the "profane" structure. The Chamber building was still thirty percent empty several months after its opening.

"Anyway," Sera declares, "I think the Dome should be torn down altogether, although I guess not many agree with me on that. It represents the tragic past, which should be forgotten. It doesn't do anything for peace . . . If they want a monument, they could make a small one with the materials from the ruin . . . You know, the Occupation authorities came around in 1948 with the idea that we preserve three ruins like that one, but I was against it when they asked my opinion. If we had done that, the whole city would have fallen into decay."

On their fortunate and prosperous perch, Sera and son fairly purr with conservative convictions. "It's not true," says Kikuo, "that everyone in Hiroshima went left because of the Bomb. Most of the *hibak'sha* are conservatives." "The so-called progressive forces," says the father, "like to use the Bomb like a sign in a store window, because it attracts customers." Hiroshima's problem of unemployment among the middle-aged "would solve itself easily enough," the elder Sera believes, "if they wouldn't worry so much about saving face and would take the jobs that are offered to them. They've got to get rid of the idea that be-

27

cause one man used to be a section chief in a company, he can't work as a sales clerk now."

Sera and son sound almost like the stereotype of the conservative businessman—but this is Hiroshima. "What happened in war cannot be helped," says the elder, sipping his tea and locking his gaze on mine. "But the Atom Bomb is different from other bombs because it kills everyone without discrimination, and it spreads radiation which keeps on killing, and when you are Atom-Bombed, there is no escape, no place to hide, no succor, nothing. No one in Hiroshima hates America any more, but America, I think, should acknowledge a spiritual responsibility at least. I don't mean that they should come here and try to compensate in any way; that's impossible. But Americans should at least feel apologetic for what they have done to the people of Hiroshima."

He paused, to weigh the effect of his words, and son Kikuo began to speak. "Some of my friends, they were very badly burned, and scarred terribly with keloids. They could not get good jobs. I'm thinking of one friend in particular. He was very bright, graduated number one in our class, and certainly would have got a good job in a big firm. But just because his face was scarred, he couldn't get a top job, and they told him frankly he was not being hired because

28

of his 'bad appearance.' He's working now, but it's a second-rank firm, nothing near what he deserves."

Kikuo looked at his father, squirmed a bit in embarrassment, and went on. "You know, my father's children were born before the Bomb dropped. He doesn't really appreciate what makes the Atom Bomb different. The effect of this Bomb doesn't end in one generation. I was terribly worried when my wife bore our children. I had absorbed the Bomb and I didn't know whether I would have normal children, or what would happen. They are normal healthy boys, who are now—let's see—nine and seven. But this is just the beginning. It doesn't end with my generation. We don't know what will happen in the next generation, and the grandchildren. That's what makes the A-Bomb different."

A friend of the elder Sera, another Hondori shopkeeper, had joined us around the low table. One of the shopgirls had brought us more tea and some little pink sweetpastes on tiny lacquered trays. We sat on cushions laid on a flowered yellow carpet spread over the traditional *tatami* mat floor, and listened to the murmur of commerce from the store out front and from the bustling Hondori beyond. The young man's words had been followed by silence, as the four of us contemplated the future. It was time for me to leave, and I began the rigmarole of farewell courtesies.

But something remained unsaid in the air, another impression they wanted me to take away, like a sweet tea after a bitter one. The friend finally put it in words. "Right after the Bomb, you know, we never thought things would be so good so soon." The Seras, father and son, nodded vigorously and uttered assent, and the other man finished: "It says something good, after all, about the greatness and strength of people, of what they can do."

Except for the Dome there is nothing in the aspect of Hiroshima that says "Atom Bomb." The city is clean, bright and airy, with wide boulevards and stretches of green belt along the river, and the old castle that was knocked down by the blast has been reconstructed. The slums and shantytowns appear to be just small blemishes on the face of the city. The city looks new, because it is, and fresh, because it is still a-building, and only around the edges, here and there, does one notice that parts of it are jerry-built and cheap, and aging before their time. A visitor from abroad, dropped suddenly into the Kamiya-cho intersection, just three hundred meters from the hypocenter (the spot directly under the explosion), would have no means of guessing where in Japan he was—unless he were shrewd enough to note that the streets are eight or ten lanes wide.

Hiroshima is small in area, only thirty-three square miles cupped in the hills ringing the Ota estuary, but with a population of 522,685 it is Japan's eleventh city. Mayor Hamai is proud of the fact that "unlike other urban areas in Japan we have been able to fulfill almost our entire city plan."

To do it, 21,000 shanties that survivors had hammered together out of debris in the first months after the Bomb were demolished or moved, and practically every street in the burnt-out central area was shifted or widened or altered in some way. So much property was swapped and purchased and expropriated without much thought of relative value, in order to widen and pave streets and build roads, bridges and parks, that by the end of 1965 city and prefectural authorities had not yet begun to even out the accounts. Some landowners will be compensated with cash or extra land, and some will have to pay the government because the property they received turned out to be more valuable than the land they had to give up. But the process is slow and full of controversy, for the city is not the complete master of its house. When reconstruction started, the city government asked the prefectural authorities for financial assistance. "We thought it would be better," recalls Mayor Hamai, "for the city to do the whole thing as one unit, and asked for money for that purpose. However, the prefectural governor of that time said that instead of giving us the money he would send workers and administrators, and help us do the job."

Looking across the shantytown of 1949 to the City Hall, the conservative governor had seen a municipal administration hamstrung by machine control of the City Council, and under the command of an untried "progressive," young Mayor Hamai, who first took office in 1947 at the age of thirty-seven. Two political bosses were building thriving machines on the basis of their effective lobbying for *hibak'sha* assistance laws, and later, one was even elected to a Council seat while under arrest on a kickback charge. The task of reconstruction seemed too huge for the city; the Prefecture took over the entire responsibility for executing the city plan on the west side, and city authorities managed the rest. Final reckoning on the land transfers has been delayed because the two governments disagree over how much to assess property owners.

The prefectural governor clearly underestimated Mayor Hamai and the municipal staff. Hamai is an immensely popular political independent who has turned down bids to join both the conservative Liberal Democrats and the Socialists. As a recognized "progressive" interested in the Peace Movement, he could count on the support of the unions and the Socialists. And the respectable conservatives backed him to prevent the machine from taking over completely. The bosses in the City Council could, and can, frequently delay the mayor's more ambitious plans, but they did not prevent him from building the city more or less the way he and the planners saw it.

"We are proud of the way we all worked together, in the early days, when everyone was only interested in getting enough to eat," says Mayor Hamai. Today it seems that all the fine new buildings lie to the east of the Peace Park, and all the unpaved streets and most of the slums to the west. But, the mayor concedes, the city was growing eastward even before the war, and the Bomb just gave it an extra shove; when the old market area in the west side was destroyed, Hiroshima found it more convenient to start a new one near the railroad station on the east. What gives the eastern section its air of modernity is a construction code that insists on fireproof steel-and-concrete buildings along all the main streets. Builders get government subsidies for putting up such structures more than three stories high—one reason for the surfeit of office space. The same code and subsidies apply to the west, but fewer builders take advantage of it, and it is not so strictly enforced.

East and west, the city has developed so quickly that a new, grander Hiroshima Regional Plan "that we never dreamed we would need," according to one civic engineer, is now being drafted. "But already industrialization in the surrounding area is proceeding so fast that our regional planning is far behind." "Government circles, both central and local," says the official city handbook, "now visualize Hiroshima as the prospective center of a greatly extended economic sphere reaching out as far as [fifty miles] in all directions from Hiroshima and covering all of the four surrounding prefectures."

Straddling the city limits on the eastern outskirts, the Toyo Kogyo auto plant, Hiroshima's biggest factory, demonstrates the rapidity of industrialization in Hiroshima and the progress of Japanese manufacturing. In the 1930's Toyo was a small plant that produced motorcycles and a few tiny cars, and during the war it turned out rifles for the Imperial Army and engines for the Zero fighter. Although it was too

34

far away from the center of the city to be damaged by the Bomb, there was nothing for it to do after the war, and by the end of 1945 the work force had shrunk from 11,000 to fewer than 1,000 employees.

Ironically for the City of Peace, the Korean War rescued Hiroshima from economic stagnation. Although the company history doesn't mention it, orders for jeeps, trucks and machine-gun parts for the U.S. Army gave the company the chance to expand, and when peace came to Korea, Toyo quickly took the lead in the production of the three-wheel "motorcycle" truck, the cheap, maneuverable and hardy workhorse of Japan's economic recovery. At the same time, the company was modernizing, automating and acquiring foreign technology. Huge roomfuls of IBM computers now solve problems of body design, count the number of spare parts on hand, determine automatically what color to paint each of the 25,000 trucks and passenger cars coming off the three assembly lines every month, and keep track of the company's $100 million annual export orders. The company runs its own fleet of sixty-eight ships to transport its vehicles, and is so dedicated to automation that even in the bright new company hospital, closed-circuit television cameras monitor critical patients, and doctors' prescriptions stream along on a conveyor belt on varicolored clips for quick, efficient filling.

It is all very far from the Bomb. The company will not admit to discriminatory hiring policies, but only a tiny handful of *hibak'sha* work at the plant, and no keloid scars mar the sleek vistas of polished machinery and clean dungaree. The 19,000 people tending the humming assembly lines have been picked, for the most part, from the newcomers—many of them refugees tossed out of Japan's overseas possessions by defeat—who flowed into the city after the war, seeking opportunity and recognizing grimly that with about half of the city wiped out, there would be that much more elbowroom—and working space —for the others.

Compared to other places in Japan, the newcomers say Hiroshima is *sumi-yasui*—the living is easy. They came and settled by choice, several hundred thousand of them, and they brought with them some of the immigrant's sense of self-confidence and control of his own destiny. Free of the handicap of family tradition, free of the stigma and the illness, and the scars and terrible knowledge, of the Bomb, they give the city a cosmopolitan flavor rare in Japan. People like them can be found in Tokyo and Osaka and Nagoya, but they constitute such a large proportion of the new population of Hiroshima that they have re-made the character of the city.

Junichiro Ishiwari is a newcomer and a newsman. "Old castle towns in Japan," he explains, "were tra-ditionally exclusive and snooty. They knew how to be polite on the surface, but strangers never really felt at home in them. Well, Hiroshima is a castle town, and even up to the war I have the feeling that it was the same way. But now all the people have changed, and it's not exclusive at all. There's a bright feeling about it, and one can make friends, real friends, easily and quickly, because the people have come from all over and they don't feel that someone is an outlander because he was born somewhere else . . . It's a good place to live. I didn't realize it be-fore I came, but as soon as I got here I could feel it, and I'd like to stay."

Hiroshima, the new parts and the main streets, sparkles and hums; there's a drive that is not found in other cities of its size in Japan, and if there is something just a little bit tawdry about it around the edges, well, it's still growing. And if the newcomers sometimes seem to ignore the terrible history of the place, maybe it is because they're callous, or maybe they know what they're doing.

37

Typical of the new breed is Kiyoshi Nakahara, a sharp, ambitious young salesman for a construction materials company, who was transferred to Hiroshima from Tokyo in 1964. "When I first came here," he recalls, "I had this idea, this impression of the Atom-Bombed city, and I looked around and went to the museum and the memorial, with something like pity for the victims and for the city itself. But now, you know, I've changed my outlook. I find that Hiroshima is a city of peace. The people don't want to be treated as something pitiful. It hurts them if you look at them that way . . . Now I don't think of Hiroshima as the Atom-Bombed city. I'm like the Hiroshima people. They don't want tourists and visitors to come here because of the A-Bomb and say, 'What a sad, pitiful city.' They want them to say, 'My, what a big, prosperous, pleasant city this is.' There is a saying, *'sumeba miyako,'* wherever you live becomes the capital. I was born and brought up in Tokyo, but now I'm living here and I like it."

The young man was protesting just a bit too much, I thought. "Take that museum," he went on. "If you ask the people of Hiroshima, they would like it to be torn down. They want to forget the terrible things that are there. Everybody thinks that." Do the sick, and the scarred, I asked him with some incredulity, also want to tear it down and forget?

The reply came quickly, and began to make sense. "As for them, we must encourage them, tell them to keep up their spirits, and to get better, and we should help them if we can. But if we say we feel sorry for them, pity them—then that's an insult. It's like when a person has an accident, and maybe loses an arm, well, he still has another arm and he has his legs, and has confidence in himself, and he doesn't want to be pitied, or babied, or have a fuss made over him. It would hurt his self-confidence. Well, that's the way the Hiroshima people feel. For instance, the men in my office. I don't know which are *hibak'sha* and which are not. They never talk about the Bomb, and I never ask. They don't want my sympathy. We are working together, doing the same work. We are equal. There should not be any special sympathy on one side or the other, or it would change our relationship of equality."

For another new citizen, Hiroshima is the big time compared to his home town. Tetsuo Sumiyama, thirty-four, came to Hiroshima five years ago from the backward northwest coast of Japan, and now programs an IBM computer for the Chugoku Electric

Power Company; his job involves research, personnel, power production and consumption. "This is the head office, this is where the planning is being done. It's a bigger job, more important. This has a future, and this is where I want to stay."

Hiroshi Kawanishi finds even more to praise in his adopted home. He was brought up in Kure, only fifteen miles from Hiroshima, and from there, as a boy, saw the mushroom cloud and watched the stricken refugees struggling in agony to get away from the blasted city. But it was not happening to him. Kure was a naval base, and later United States and British Commonwealth troops were stationed there. Kawanishi went to work as a taxi driver and prospered, but when the bases closed, the Kure economy declined, and five years ago the bushy-haired Kawanishi moved to Hiroshima, "where jobs were easy to find."

Now he no longer drives a taxi himself. He is the full-time paid chairman of a taxi-drivers' union affiliated to SOHYO, the largest and furthest left of Japan's labor federations. "Hiroshima," says this representative of the laboring left, "is only a middle-sized city, but it has most of the advantages of a metropolis: department stores, supermarkets, convenient transportation. And the people have the spirit of a big city. Places like Tokyo are foul with smog, and the rivers are filthy. It's not pleasant to live there. Here we can go fishing in the rivers, and swimming in the summertime. Nature has provided the good life. This is a place where nature has not yet been ravaged." He spoke simply and blandly, entirely unaware, as far as I could tell, of the awful irony of his words.

Along the river where Kawanishi likes to fish, just a few hundred yards downstream from the blasted Dome, the bright-colored rowboats glide past a floating restaurant moored to the bank. Hiroshima oysters, famous throughout Japan, are the specialty of the Kanawa, and *sake* and beer are plentiful on board. Kimonoed waitresses bearing trays of seafood delicacies glide along polished wood passageways, and gracefully drop to their knees before sliding open the paper doors to the airy rooms over water where guests sit on grass-fresh *tatami* mats, gazing at the deep green river, or admiring the flower arrangements in the alcoves. By day it is sunny and quiet, with a cool river breeze. In the evening, reflections from strings of colored lanterns twinkle like confetti on the water, the *sake* flows quicker, the parties are larger and louder, and *geisha* and other blossoms of the night flutter down the gangplank to the deck. Later still, from the darkened Peace Park just upstream, come the strollers two by two to board the oyster ark, some still with the grass of the hallowed ground in their hair.

Sumiko Ezuki, waitress, brings in the beer and pours the *sake* and sets out the dishes for a feast; she can make conversation, or sing an old song, and knows how to keep a tipsy customer from tipping into the river without spoiling his fun. She is young enough for her age to matter, but too old to be asked it—anyway, she remembers the old Hiroshima, which she visited often before the war from her home in the suburbs. For fifteen years now she has lived in the city itself, and watched it grow again, and poured beer for the newcomers, and let them tickle her, if such was their mood, but Sumiko is sad.

"It's a good place to live, all right; fresh food from the sea, and things from the mountains nearby too. Ah, but I miss the old Hiroshima. It was *ottori* then, calm and placid, but now everything is *gasa-gasa*, all confused and hectic, with everybody scrambling around to make money, and the streets so crowded, and everything so noisy and crude and no one polite any more. It was better before."

In front of the Peace Museum, just visible from Sumiko's delightful Kanawa, a luscious new mechanical fountain tosses gay jets of "dancing" water into the unspoiled crystal air. Technicolor spotlights render the fountain crudely splendiferous in the evening, like a tremendous liquid juke box, and the people of Hiroshima flock to stare at it in wonder. On fine Sundays the flow of the populace to and around the fountain starts early with family groups, followed by small boys on their way to play baseball, and later in the afternoon, gaggles of teen-agers and solemn, self-conscious twosomes in brand-new suits and kimonos—engaged couples on their first formal, awkward "date." The fountain, a young man declared proudly, "is the grandest thing in town," and to residents of Hiroshima, especially the newcomers, it is the lake in Central Park, Trafalgar Square, the Champs Élysées. Gasping at the rhythmic jets of water, the sprays and whorls and quivering pink parabolas, few stop to consider what the gushing display is doing there. It is, officially, the "Fountain of Prayers," offering clean fresh water forever to the thousands of A-Bomb victims who died crying their thirst in the hours and days following the blast.

On weekdays Hiroshima's *gasa-gasa* daytime scramble merges without missing a beat into the evening activities; the route from the place of making money to the places for spending it seldom touches home. Department stores, offices and workshops close around five, but small stores like those on the Hondori stay open late into the evening to soak up what they can from the pleasure-bent citizens. An evening out starts when the day's work is done and the action moves with hastening steps to the district of bars, cabarets and movie houses.

For the youth of the town, night life swirls around the Casino and the Palace dance halls, not far from Hondori. At the Casino, the poshier of the two, the multicolored haze is filled with the sounds of three bands in turn, one for Hawaiian music, one for the twist, and one for *chiiku-dansu*, cheek-to-cheek dancing. The Palace gets by with only two orchestras, but the shopgirls and the dance-hall *samurai* who go there are, say those who should know, less interested in dancing than other pursuits, so it doesn't matter. "No, we don't tell our parents that we come to the Palace," admitted one boy in an elegant suit he said was "Ivy" style.

Youngsters who probably do keep their parents informed can be found singing their lungs out at the Musica coffee house, which distributes songbooks with the fruit sundaes, and those athletically inclined go ice-skating or bowling. At eight P.M. every evening a temple bell informs middle-school students, those up to fifteen years old, that it's time to leave the area and go home.

Men of more years or substance, of course, can choose from a greater variety of entertainments, from the plush Club V, where two or three Scotches, some peanuts and about an hour's sophisticated conversation with superbly coiffed and shockingly attractive hostesses can somehow cost about twenty dollars, to the raunchy bars and cabarets where chubby country girls in too-short fluffy party skirts flounce down next to the customer and clutch his thigh all in one practiced and harmonious motion. Nobody, of course, talks about the Bomb, unless the customer insists. Most of the girls are too young to remember, and anyway, said one, "it's not good for the mood." And the number one girl in the number one club in modern Hiroshima wants to marry an American—or so she says to her American customers.

There are some nights, however, when the bars and the *pachinko* pinball arcades and the dance halls might just as well close early. That's when the Hiroshima Carps are playing a home game, and the brightest, most *gasa-gasa* spot in all Hiroshima is the Municipal Stadium across the street from the Atomic Dome. Never in fifteen years of competition have the

Carps finished better than fourth among the six teams of the Central League. But the fact that they thrive in the *donzoko,* the lower depths, or the abyss, as the Japanese league cellar is called, only makes their hysterical fans more fiercely partisan and violent.

It's a little bit like the old days of the Dodgers in Brooklyn. Even the arch-enemies bear the same name, the Giants, and tickets for all Giant games in Hiroshima are sold out months in advance. No matter who the opponents may be, however, Carp fans are easily provoked to roughhouse and riot, and visiting players sometimes need police protection. On one memorable occasion, after a freak triple play of the kind "that could only happen in Flatbush," umpires and managers argued for two and a half hours about a disputed decision, while the fans grew restive, and then called the game off. That brought a thousand spectators boiling out of their seats, attacking umpires, setting fire to benches, tearing down the screen behind home plate and ripping out lighting and television equipment. When riot police tried to escort the visiting Hanshin Tiger team to its bus, they found all the bus seats occupied by jeering, hooting Hiroshima fans.

Some months later the Tigers were again in Hiroshima, and the police arrested a Tiger fan for carrying a long, wicked knife. He was let off with a stern warning when he explained that "lots of Hanshin fans bring knives when they come to Hiroshima, in order to protect our players. It's dangerous for them in this town."

One reason that Hiroshima is Japan's noisiest and most enthusiastic baseball city may be the fact that stock in the Carp club is public, and thousands of citizens own a chunk of it. The stock is profitable too: only two Japanese baseball teams make money, the Carps and the Giants.

But the ready violence, many believe, is a hangover from the era of lawlessness and gangsterism that Hiroshima endured in the years immediately after the Bomb, when the social fabric had been ripped apart and everyone depended on his wits and his strength to stay alive. The Bomb set thousands of homeless orphans loose in the ruins, and before the authorities could round them up to care for them, many had found their way into the black market, and later into organized gangs. Although police crackdowns and the passage of time have eliminated the more flagrant marks of gang rule, more organized *yakuza* still rumble through the streets of Hiroshima than in other small cities in Japan, and peace is preserved today very largely because one gang, the Yamagura-*gumi*, finally fought its way to dominance over the others, and then reorganized as a "political party."

Gasa-gasa though the city may be, not everyone longs for the old days. Elderly Dr. Kenji Tsuboi, a retired physician, rebuilt his practice quickly after the war and achieved considerable wealth. Hiroshima, he says, "is better off than before the war. There's more food, better clothing and a better life for more people. But there is something new: there's a greater gap between the livelihood of rich and poor than we used to see. Now those who are prosperous, like me, live very well indeed," and from his big, comfortable armchair in a room studded with expensive art work, he waved his hand at his classic Japanese garden. "But there are still people living in shacks," he went on. "Housing, in fact, is our one outstanding problem. It's a problem all over Japan, it's true, but it's worse here because we started from zero."

The city plan and the widened streets and the new modernity have gone only so far, and represent only part of the total picture. The other part stretches along some of the river banks, where, on land marked as green belt on the planners' maps, thousands of ragpickers, casual laborers and petty hoodlums squat in shanties as squalid and ramshackle as the worst of Japan's big-city slums. They cannot be evicted forcefully for the simple reason that the city has no place to put them, and they resist all attempts to persuade them to leave their illegal homes in the hope that some day the city might decide to buy them out.

Seven small municipal apartment houses have been constructed over the years, but these can't even accommodate a significant portion of the city's legitimate tenants, who have priority. The legal tenants are the 40,000 people of Motomachi—an area where the Japanese Army II Corps had its wartime headquarters—who have been living in flimsy three-room wooden houses that the city constructed as temporary emergency quarters in the first desperate winter after the Bomb. Here there is no running water, no city gas, no pavement. Rent to the city averages about seventy-five cents a month. Electricity is available, and many of the little houses have television, which in modern Japan is not luxury but luxury's substitute. Some Motomachi residents must turn down the chance to move to the new apartments which are being built for them on the edge of the neighborhood because they can't afford the minimum monthly rent of about five dollars. Motomachi itself was laid out as a park in the original city plan, but in the face of necessity that was changed and now the whole area is projected for apartments. It will take ten more years to finish the job unless additional sources of city funds can be found.

Only about fifteen percent of the Motomachi residents are *hibak'sha,* but thousands of other survivors live in similar poverty, or worse, in other areas. At present, 93,211 of Hiroshima's 522,687 citizens hold survivors' registration books, less than one fifth, but *hibak'sha* families make up one third of the municipal relief rolls. More than forty percent of the unemployed who occasionally get work on city projects for the poor are people who "saw the *pika.*" "It is clear," says a welfare official, "that for reasons of illness, or because all the breadwinners and potential breadwinners were wiped out in one blow, many survivor families never made their postwar recovery."

It is only a ten-minute stroll from the crowded, dusty penury of Motomachi, past the Dome, to the picnic mood of the Park of Peace. Some of the squatters on the river bank can even stare at the frolic from their windows on the water. The children of Hiroshima, as the lady from Wisconsin noted, are enjoying themselves; the adults are taking pictures.

Throughout the park, the cameras click away like busy Geiger counters, filling up thousands of albums with thousands of identical poses of small stiff groups in front of the cenotaph, the museum, the sportive fountain. But sometimes a particular photo will assume prophetic and fateful significance.

One such picture, snapped on a sunny January Sunday, catches an ordinary-looking middle-class Japanese family: a chubby two-year-old boy clumping with obvious glee across the grass of the park; a proud, handsome father in a sporty tweed coat; and, keeping slightly to the rear of her husband and son as a good Japanese wife must do, the smiling, dazzling young mother, in flowered kimono and *haori*. It is a peaceful, pleasant, happy photo, and, like similar snapshots in family albums all over the world, it would tug a warm smile out of anyone—except that directly behind and above the figure of the mother rises the skeleton of the Atomic Dome in a white winter sky. For the Sato family of Fukuyama in the suburbs of Hiroshima, that was an omen of tragedy.

3 ⁂

Mrs. Harue Sato smiled wanly when I asked about her family. Her thin white hand delicately drew the snapshot from a drawer by her bedside and, with care, held it out to me. Some months had passed since that Sunday in the Peace Park, and now Mrs. Sato lay abed in Hiroshima's Atom Bomb Hospital, slowly dying of leukemia.

Harue was ten years old when the Bomb exploded 1,300 yards away from her. She grew up apparently healthy, let her hair grow long and lovely, and studied hard. At Hiroshima Junior College she majored in English literature, read Dickens and even some Shakespeare. In history class, she learned about the war. For a while she taught English to neighborhood children and later worked in an exporter's office, translating business letters, but she was always too modest to use her English with foreigners who spoke Japanese. In 1961 she married a salesman of *futon*, Japanese quilts, and a year later her son, Fumitaka, was born. In the spring of 1963, when Fumitaka was ten months old, Harue Sato entered the Atom Bomb Hospital, complaining of general weakness. The doctors found an enlarged spleen and an abnormal increase of white blood cells. They didn't tell her what they knew even then, what they had seen so tragically often before: that leukemia, the first disease proven to have been caused by A-Bomb radiation, was going to kill her. The war was no longer history.

Mrs. Sato spent four months in the hospital that spring, and then, following a now classic pattern, recovered enough to go home. But the following year, again in the spring, she had to enter the hospital once more, and that time she stayed five months. In 1965, a few months after the photo in the park was taken, she had been hospitalized again because, she told me with a hopeful smile, "the condition has not quite cleared up. We have a saying in Hiroshima, *'Ki-no-me tatsu, warui.'* When the buds come out, unlucky." In the endless hours, staring at the ceiling of her hospital room, she was worrying about her boy and her husband and how they were getting along without her. "Just one day sooner, if I could get out just one day sooner, it would make such a difference, to bring us together again." Still she had not been told she was suffering from leukemia, and if she guessed, she was keeping her fears to herself, to spare her family. Before he let me speak with her, Dr. Fumio Shigeto, the director of the hospital, had exacted my promise not to mention the name of her disease.

In June, a few weeks after I spoke to her, Harue Sato did go home to her husband and child. "But her remissions are getting shorter," Dr. Shigeto commented, and he knew he would see her soon again. The end, when it came, was quick. She re-entered the hospital on September 10, 1965, and died, aged thirty, two days later.

There were five leukemia patients in the Atom Bomb Hospital when I visited it. Seventeen more *hibak'sha* were suffering from ills in a category legally, but not medically, defined as "Atom Bomb diseases." The other 83 *hibak'sha* in the hospital had ordinary illnesses. Since the hospital opened in 1956, 54 *hibak'sha* have died there of leukemia. All told, 176 survivors of the Bomb died in Hiroshima of leukemia during that period, while only 109 persons in the non-exposed population were succumbing to the disease, although the non-exposed population is five times as great.

Funds raised by the Japanese Post Office, through the sale of special New Year cards, paid for the construction of the hospital and its Nagasaki counterpart; and the institution is administered by the Japanese Red Cross Hospital, which adjoins it and which Dr. Shigeto also directs. For all *hibak'sha* who were within 3,000 meters of the hypocenter at the time of the *pika,* the Japanese government pays all medical expenses for all illnesses. "This is because," Dr. Shigeto explains, "it takes these people longer to get well, as they are generally in weak condition." Regardless of illness, any *hibak'sha* can come to the A-Bomb Hospital, or can go to any hospital or doctor he chooses and still receive government assistance. Cancer patients, Dr. Shigeto explains, generally go to the Hiroshima University Hospital, which specializes in tumors. "But those who have scars," says Dr. Shigeto, "usually come here anyway."

A stubby, baldish man with bushy brows and an undisciplined mustache, Dr. Shigeto moves and speaks with an air of steadfast calm and simplicity. Although he can discuss with cool clinical precision the medical aspects of a case, he is equally deliberate and thorough in setting out the human and emotional elements. He knows and cares almost as much about his patients' personalities and private problems as

55

about their medical histories; he proceeds through the corridors and wards like dawn breaking across the land; the gloomy faces open into smiles, and hope seems to come alive. It is not pity he shows the sick, but understanding, and he comes by it naturally, and they know.

In one room on the third floor Dr. Shigeto pointed out to me a tiny girl, the height and weight of a twelve-year-old, with the head and face of a child of nine and not enough intellect to get through the first grade. She was nineteen. "Microcephalic. She was *in utero*, fourth month, and about 950 meters from the Bomb. There were many cases like this. The growing foetus is particularly susceptible to radiation. Now she has blood trouble. No, not leukemia, but it could lead to that." He smiled at the girl. "She speaks, understands, takes care of herself and walks around, but couldn't manage at all in school." He paused, turned away. "Cute kid, though."

In another room he indicated an elderly man, exposed at 1,500 meters, who had been in the hospital two years earlier with a different complaint and whose blood at that time was normal. "Even now," he said, "twenty years after the *pika*, there are people who suddenly come down with leukemia, although they had never shown any signs of it before.

When this man came in this time with leukemia, we couldn't believe it, we thought we must have made a mistake the first time we saw him. But we re-checked the blood sample from two years ago and we had been right. There was nothing there." The doctor switched to slow, careful English, for the patient was now watching us. "He won't live long. I never heard that any adult survived leukemia." We walked off down the hall and he slipped back into Japanese. "It's hearing about that kind of case that makes some *hibak'sha* frantic with worry if they just have a headache or a nosebleed."

Downstairs in his office, over cups of tea, Dr. Shigeto explained the grim statistics. Among Japanese in general, the leukemia rate is only about two or three per 100,000 of population per year, but among *hibak'sha* who were within 3,000 meters of the blast, it has at times been as high as fifteen per 100,000, still hovers around eight, and is again rising slightly, "contrary to our expectations." For persons who were closest to the explosion, the rate is even more dramatic. Between 1,000 and 1,500 meters, it rises to about 50 per 100,000 and for those exposed within 1,000 meters it is 200, thus leaving no doubt in the minds of scientists that the Bomb is responsible.

A few years ago, according to the doctor, there

was an unexpected increase in leukemia cases among survivors who had been further than 2,000 meters from the explosion, and the Survivors' Medical Assistance Law was amended to give *hibak'sha* up to 3,000 meters from the hypocenter the right to free medical care. Others who came into the city in the first few days and breathed the ionized air have contracted lung cancer, as well as leukemia, he says, and they too have now been given "special" *hibak'sha* registration books.

"Special" *hibak'sha* status and free care are also granted to survivors suffering from any of the legally recognized "A-Bomb diseases," regardless of how far from the center they were on August 6th. These diseases—leukemia, cancers, aplastic anemia and liver and endocrine disturbances—"we suppose are connected with radiation," says Dr. Shigeto, "but except for leukemia and thyroid cancer, they have not been scientifically proven to be induced by the Bomb." American scientists tend to bristle at the term "A-Bomb disease," because, strictly speaking, there is no such thing—all of the diseases also occur in people who have never been near a nuclear explosion. And they complain, privately, when the Japanese press lists as a Bomb victim every *hibak'sha* who succumbs to cancer or anemia, because the connection has not been definitely established. But the attitude of the Japanese Welfare Ministry seems to be that as long as there is a likelihood that the Bomb caused some of these cases—and no one denies the possibility—then the patients are entitled to the same assistance that leukemia victims get. It wouldn't do them any good if they were to die for lack of care before the scientists prove their case. The objection to this attitude is purely one of public relations: not only does the Japanese press play up every death as caused by the Bomb, but the names of all *hibak'sha* who die from these diseases are added to the list of Bomb victims under the Peace Park cenotaph, and the majority of Japanese assume that "A-Bomb disease" means just that.

As the *hibak'sha* grow older, the rates of death and illness naturally rise; the 120 beds in the A-Bomb Hospital are usually full and fifty more beds are about to be added. Still, Shigeto and many other officials complain that not enough is being done. Hundreds of *hibak'sha* out-patients really belong in a hospital bed, but although the treatment is free, they and their families can't afford to have them stop working. They should get special assistance, Dr. Shigeto feels, "and the government should also do something for the badly scarred *hibak'sha* who never leave their homes, who cannot marry or hold jobs. It is thought that if a person is healthy, he or she can work no matter how badly scarred, but in practice it just doesn't work out that way."

Those scarred lightly—and by Hiroshima standards that means those who can be looked at by the strong-stomached without revulsion—do come to the hospital. Even as the doctor spoke, a new patient was being admitted, and a little later I talked to her. She sat up in bed, hunched over as if trying to hide the keloids on her face and neck, and busied herself sewing a bed jacket. Her left hand stayed out of sight beneath the bed covers, holding the cloth she was working on. Her name was Setsuko Yoshimura; she was thirty-six and unmarried. She had entered the hospital for observation and diagnosis, complaining of heart palpitations.

With an embarrassed smile, Miss Yoshimura related what she had apparently told often in the past. "I was waiting at Hiroshima Station for a train to Okayama. The train was late, probably because of the air-raid alarm that had sounded earlier. I think if it had not been late I would have been well out of the city when the Bomb fell . . . I saw the plane, the B-29. I put my hand over my eyes to look at it, like this"—and her left hand, still twisted and grotesquely misshapen, darted out from under the sheet and flitted to her brow for an instant—"and then there was a bright flash, and I dove under a baggage cart on the platform." She sighed. "And when it was over, I ran home." And that is all, obviously, that she wants to say.

Her hand at her brow had saved her eyes, and she had ducked the force of the blast, but her hand, face and body were irradiated. In the corridor, her mother and her married sister were waiting to talk to the doctors. "When she got home," her sister remembers, "her face was covered with burns, with the skin coming off. It was my own little sister, but I didn't recognize her." Later, skin was grafted from her stomach, and she spent a year and a half in bed, but finally she was able to get up, and had been working as an accountant, in a small electrical shop right near the station where she was bombed, until she fell sick. "But she could never marry," says the mother, a frail old lady in kimono, "because she can't manage a house that way." It seemed that the explanation was an excuse, worked out long ago to spare scarred Setsuko the humiliation of failing to find a husband.

We talked awhile, the family and I, and then I asked about the Dome. "It should remain as it is," the sister replied, and Mother Yoshimura nodded.

"People should see it. We want to show it"—and she bowed, to apologize for speaking so frankly—"to people from your country."

As I left the ward, Dr. Shigeto was at the nurses' office, examining the admission documents for Setsuko Yoshimura. "I see she was at the railroad station," he said softly. "That's where I was. I escaped through the station. I thought I was fairly well shielded by concrete but my blood, you know, it's not normal either. I have a low white blood count myself." Which is one reason, perhaps, why Dr. Shigeto knows his patients so well.

But because he's a medical man, Dr. Shigeto is free of the panic that some *hibak'sha* feel at every nosebleed. And he doesn't seem to suffer from the weakness, *malaise* and susceptibility to ordinary diseases that is popularly supposed to be the lot of all persons exposed to heavy radiation. "Doctors say I'm not sick, but I get tired so easily," countless *hibak'sha* report. "I have never regained the vigor I used to have." There is no medical proof that the Bomb itself is responsible for that condition, and American doctors at the Atomic Bomb Casualty Commission (A.B.C.C.) are skeptical. They believe that if it is true that *hibak'sha* are weaker than other people, it may have just as much to do with the severe malnutrition, lack of ordinary medical care and other hardships most of them suffered in the early postwar years as with the radiation from the Atom Bomb itself. But no one has ever researched the problem thoroughly.

The A.B.C.C., occupying a complex of Quonset-style buildings on the hill called Hijiyama, is a research institution, not a hospital for treatment, and its doctors are required to maintain a certain clinical and scientific detachment. The U.S. Atomic Energy Commission and Japan's National Institute of Health co-sponsor the organization, and the forty American doctors and technicians work closely in both Atom-Bombed cities with a Japanese staff of hundreds of doctors, nurses and administrative personnel. But most of the institution's funds come from the United States, the director is an American, and the Japanese regard it as an American organization. Many Japanese also complain that the A.B.C.C., pleading scientific caution, has deliberately minimized the effects of the Bomb. This the A.B.C.C. emphatically denies.

In the early days, the A.B.C.C. did not publish its findings in Japanese, and the Occupation authorities frequently suppressed reports about A-Bomb after-effects. Consequently, the Japanese were convinced that the United States was concealing some frightening statistics. For the past few years A.B.C.C. reports have been published in both languages, and the early distrust of the A.B.C.C. has slowly dissolved. Nevertheless, the impression persists among Hiroshima *hibak'sha* that the A.B.C.C. and the A.E.C., perhaps in honest fear of sensational newspaper reports, and perhaps in order to avoid alarming the survivors, do their best to hush up or delay reports of the most disturbing discoveries.

Japanese doctors, for example, have long been certain that the Bomb was responsible for an increase in certain types of cancer, but for many years the A.B.C.C. refused to concede publicly that the Bomb had induced anything other than leukemia and eye cataracts. As early as 1960, however, an authoritative A.B.C.C. official admitted privately to a reporter that the cancer rate was four times higher among Hiroshima survivors who were within 1,000 meters of the explosion than among the general Japanese population. Three years later a team of A.B.C.C. doctors reported in an American medical journal that thyroid cancer "was demonstrated to be significantly more prevalent among patients who were heavily exposed to ionizing radiation at the time of the atomic bombings in 1945." For some reason, and contrary to the usual practice, this conclusion was omitted when the data were published by the A.B.C.C. itself. Not until March of 1965 did the U.S. Atomic Energy Commission, in its annual report, announce "a small but apparently significant increase" in thyroid cancer among the survivors in both cities. By that time A.B.C.C. scientists in Hiroshima were reporting on-the-record, but still not formally publishing, the "statistically significant" increase in the total cancer rate of A-Bomb survivors.

One reason for the scientists' caution was—and is —the difficulty of measuring the exact amount of gamma rays and neutrons received by each individual. First of all, the precise radioactive "yield" of the Hiroshima uranium bomb was not known with any precision until recently, and scientists in the United States are still experimenting with nuclear reactors in an effort to refine the figures further.

Some years back, at the Nevada testing ground, the United States detonated what was in effect a replica of the Nagasaki plutonium weapon, and measured not only its yield but the degree of protection offered by various Japanese construction materials. But so complex is a nuclear reaction that even these data did not give the scientists a final figure.

More important, the exact point of detonation of the Hiroshima bomb, the epicenter, has never been satisfactorily located. From extensive shadow surveys carried out by both Japanese and American engineers soon after the war, scientists know that the epicenter was somewhere between 550 and 606 meters above the ground, and over a spot that has been determined to within a radius of 30 or 40 meters in any direction. The degree of accuracy is insufficient. How much protection a person received from a wall or other object would naturally depend on precisely where the rays came from. As long as the radiation dose each *hibak'sha* absorbed is uncertain, the doctors will be handicapped in their search for final understanding of the A-Bomb effects.

In 1965 joint Japanese-American investigating teams of the A.B.C.C. were still in the last stages of a massive attempt to determine the radiation dose received by 40,000 *hibak'sha*. Equipped with maps and charts and wartime aerial photographs, they painstakingly interviewed each of the survivors to find out exactly where he was at the moment of the *pika,* and to figure out from that how much shielding he received from surrounding objects.

Despite the limited data, A.B.C.C. doctors have recognized for many years that the Bomb caused leukemia, which is a form of cancer. Dr. Warner F. Sheldon, an A.B.C.C. pathologist, explains that leukemia was the first cancer to appear because the bone marrow which manufactures blood "is particularly sensitive to radiation." Other tumors and cancers take many years to develop and may not yet have been detected. "We will have to continue looking for cancers for the next ten or twenty years, although I will be surprised if many develop," says Sheldon. Since the thyroid is not particularly sensitive, Dr. Sheldon is "still surprised at the thyroid findings."

As thyroid cancer is very rare, only a handful of cases have been enough to show up in the statistics. Other cancers are so numerous anyway that not until a great number of cases are studied will the doctors have a clear picture of how many may have been caused by the Bomb. But they are sure that there has been an increase within the exposed portion of the "fixed population" of 100,000 people, exposed and non-exposed, that they are studying.

"When we see a patient, or when we perform an autopsy," says Dr. Sheldon, "we do not know if the individual is in the exposed group or not. We make it a rule not to know." The A.B.C.C. reports that about eighty percent of the people on its list show up for their periodic checks, and cites this as firm evidence that the people of Hiroshima are co-operating. Doctors are permitted to conduct post-mortems on about half of those on the list who die. "For the rest," says Sheldon, "we have to rely on the death certificates, and as only about a fifth die in hospital, we are never too sure about our data."

Another American pathologist has conducted chemical tests on certain tissues of survivors, and his results "suggest the presence of accelerated aging" among persons closest to the Bomb. Sheldon and other A.B.C.C. doctors tend to doubt the conclusions of that experiment, but an A.B.C.C. statistician, Dr. Antonio Ciocco, reports that *hibak'sha* who survived the initial effects of the blast and were alive in 1950, and who have died since then, lost about a half year of life on the average, compared to the non-exposed population. But, says Dr. Ciocco, "the difference in life span between rich and poor is greater than the difference between exposed and non-exposed." In Hiroshima, wealth assures, on an average, one extra year of life.

The earliest fears about the medical effects of the Bomb were that descendants of survivors would be born monsters, and the first American research doctor sent to the scene was a young geneticist, Army Lieutenant James Neel. The frightening numbers of abnormal births in the first nine months after the atomic bombing—births of embryos exposed to radiation *in utero,* like Mrs. Hamada's boy and the microcephalic girl in the hospital—had terrified the people of the Atom-Bombed cities, many of whom did not distinguish between injuries to growing embryos and genetic damage that could cause mutations in future generations.

Dr. Neel, now Chairman of the Department of Human Genetics at University of Michigan, still visits Hiroshima and Nagasaki as an A.B.C.C. consultant from time to time, but the seven-year study he conducted jointly with other scientists has considerably calmed the jittery population—without proving or disproving that mutations took place. To determine the extent of genetic damage, Neel and his colleagues examined 80,000 newborn babies in Hiroshima and Nagasaki, about ninety-three percent of all births. So that no abnormalities would be hidden from them by frightened and ashamed parents, they paid midwives a fee to report every approaching confinement and also took the precaution of registering every woman who applied for the supplementary ration book issued to pregnant mothers.

About a tenth of the infants they saw had at least one parent who had been within 2,000 meters of the hypocenter of the Bomb. But this group, according to the A.B.C.C. report, did not show proportionately more abnormalities, stillbirths, infant mortality or cases of underweight babies than the children of un-exposed parents. The only genetic effect discovered was a change in the sex ratio: irradiated fathers produced fewer daughters and irradiated mothers bore fewer boys. This change itself was consistent with the doctors' assumption that lethal mutations had taken place. But as for further genetic damage, either the mutations were so incompatible with life that conception was impossible altogether, or the rate of increased abnormalities and stillbirths was too small for the limited sample to detect.

"Man cannot be an exception," says Neel. "There is no doubt that radiation produces mutations; it has done so in every animal. But to demonstrate that it happened in Nagasaki and Hiroshima is extremely difficult. Therefore, saying that we only found a change in the sex ratio does not mean that nothing else happened. And although we cannot demonstrate an increase in abnormality, we cannot, statistically, rule out the possibility that a small increase did take place. What we *can* say, with some certainty, is that the malformation rate was not double the normal rate and that the stillbirths did not increase more than 1.8 times." That is to say, assuming that one out of a hundred births are, in ordinary circumstances, abnormal, then among *hibak'sha* the number of such births could not have been more than two per hundred. "This means," says another doctor, "that for the individual the added risk is small, although for society as a whole the potential damage could be considerable."

The examination of newborn infants ended years ago, and no similar study is planned for the second generation, but the A.B.C.C. in 1965 began investigating all deaths of children under ten years old in a search for hidden and delayed lethal mutations.

The mutation fears have faded, at least for this generation. Most *hibak'sha*, anyway, have passed through the fertile years to enter the cancer age, and now have a new set of worries. They get jumpy at the slightest pain and read the reports of cancer deaths at the A-Bomb Hospital with morbid fascination. Yet such are the social pressures that there are some who don't show up for official blood tests and health checks when special city medical teams come around to their neighborhoods twice a year. "Many of them," says a doctor on one of these teams, "don't like to ask time off from work for this purpose as long as they feel all right. They don't like their employers to know that they are *hibak'sha*." And Dr. Shigeto points out: "None of our statistics on leukemia, or

71

any other disease, are perfectly reliable. A lot of people, of course, said they were closer than they really were in order to benefit from the medical assistance law. But there were others who did not want to register at all because it is sometimes difficult to get jobs or get married if it is known that you are *hibak'sha.*"

For years badly scarred survivors were barred from some public bathhouses, the center of Japanese community life, because they disgusted the other customers. When jobs were scarce, anyone known to have been exposed to radiation was practically unemployable, because of the chance that he might be too weak and sickly to work steadily. More fortunate survivors and unscrupulous newcomers ruthlessly exploited the down-and-out, and frequently even tried to steal the property of the dead. Meanwhile, Occupation authorities were censoring all mention of radiation aftereffects and banning books and photographs depicting too dreadfully the experiences of Hiroshima and Nagasaki. And not until 1949, with encouragement from General MacArthur's headquarters, did the Japanese parliament get around to voting extra funds for the reconstruction of the two Atom-Bombed cities; not until 1957 did it pass the first Survivors' Medical Assistance Law.

The *hibak'sha* response was the natural one: those

that could, hid their scars and their experiences, especially if they had health and work. Many who couldn't, who were ill or unemployed, joined the ranks of what soon came to be called the "professional *hibak'sha*," who signed every "appeal," gave frequent interviews, or let their keloids be photographed time and again. Other Hiroshima residents accused them of "peddling their scars"—especially as it became obvious that they were being exploited for political reasons. But even some of the heroes of John Hersey's *Hiroshima* were shunned by neighbors and colleagues (when the Occupation finally allowed the volume to be translated after a three-year delay), because they had achieved undeserved personal fame. "We all suffered," say those who did. "Why should one or two get all the attention?" Nagasaki survivors crack sarcastic about Hiroshima's unequal share of the publicity, choosing to ignore the fact that Hiroshima also received an unequally large share of the damage and casualties.* And Hiroshima city officials complain pleasantly about foreign magazine articles which

* The Nagasaki bomb fell more than two miles from the aiming point, and intervening hills saved the central part of the city from destruction. Estimates of Nagasaki A-Bomb deaths range from 35,000 to 74,000. The area of "complete destruction" was 1.45 square miles in Nagasaki, and 4.7 square miles in Hiroshima.

quote average individuals who are neither leaders nor well-known people, wondering why such insignificant residents of Hiroshima have been singled out.

The Hiroshima fear of being labeled a "pro," of attracting personal attention, sometimes blocks the outsider who tries to understand the *hibak'sha* predicament. So does the traditional Japanese courtesy to guests, particularly foreign guests. Bitterness is often masked with a smile, and where there may be enmity and even hatred, the foreign visitor sometimes cannot detect it through the fog of platitudes, for candor is not a virtue and rudeness is inexcusable. "Even the American 'humanists' who fall all over themselves to apologize and show pity, never get the full story," says one Japanese who works daily with the Bomb victims. "That kind of visitor is too easily shocked, and the *hibak'sha* see this and hold back."

So it sometimes requires heavy applications of smiles and silences, of patience and time, to find out what the people of Hiroshima are really thinking and not what they believe is proper to tell. Then, if the visitor is lucky, and if no Japanese are around, his friend may reveal more in a few moments than he would even to his compatriots in a lifetime. Because once the barriers of courtesy are removed, talking to

74

a foreigner can be almost like a soliloquy—it doesn't really count in the Japanese scheme of things.

Thus, it took a while before Manabu Nakai, the thirty-three-year-old proprietor of the Bar Yodel on Nagarekawa Street, spoke up candidly. Nakai-san might have been a ruggedly handsome man if, for instance, the sky over Hiroshima had been overcast on the morning of August 6, 1945. As it is, he bears the claw mark of the blast: the left side of his face is shiny and slightly pink, with a few unnatural creases in it, and his lower lip protrudes slightly and tilts to the left, as if he were holding a fat cigar in that corner of his mouth. "I have had plastic surgery operations to take off the keloids," he says. "Luckily, I was only hurt on the outside, and I'm not so terribly ugly."

I had spoken at length to Nakai-san several times, on evenings when business was slow and we were alone in his tiny bar in the entertainment quarter. He had told of the day of the Bomb, and that his parents had survived too, and of how he had been lucky after the war to move to the mountains "where I breathed ozone and grew up healthy, not like the kids who had to live in smoggy cities." Nakai is still a fresh-air enthusiast, a mountain-climber on Sundays, and an occasional skier. That's why he chose "Yodel" as the

75

name of his bar, decorated it with photographs and paintings of Alpine scenery, and stocked his record shelf with what is probably the most extensive collection of stereo yodeling records and Tyrolean folk songs in all of western Japan.

He had told me of going to work in a restaurant in Tokyo for a few years, and of returning to Hiroshima because he wanted neither the pity nor the discrimination against *hibak'sha* that he found in the capital. "They looked at me with veiled eyes, and felt sorry, and asked me lots of questions about the *pika*. But I didn't want to talk about those things right away. I went there to work, and I wanted to show that I could do the job regardless of the fact that I had come from Hiroshima." In this he had succeeded, but had finally come back to the more "congenial" atmosphere of his home town.

And he had spoken, rather deprecatingly, I thought, of "those people in bed," the survivors who blame the Bomb for all their ills. Rather than the Bomb, he thought, it was the unhealthy life and atmosphere in postwar Hiroshima that made them weak and ill; they would have been all right if they had been brought up in the mountains as he had, he implied. He seemed to be, in this sense, a living example of the

A.B.C.C. contention that postwar environment was nearly as damaging to health as the Bomb itself.

In those early conversations Nakai the barkeep seemed to exemplify the new Hiroshima: eyes on the future, at peace with the world, concerned with business, leisure and progress. He urged me to write about the city's rebirth, saying, "This is an example of what the human spirit can do." The Bomb was all in the past, he said, and those who still harbor bitterness are in the minority. And then, over a bottle of Suntory beer late one rainy night, Manabu Nakai, bomb victim, bartender—and bachelor—started to talk.

For the first time he told me about his elder sister Chizue, who had died of leukemia nineteen years after exposure to the Bomb, although she too had gone to live in the mountains. It may have been the memory of Chizue which set him to talking, because she had died just one year and three days before our conversation and he had certainly attended a Buddhist memorial service on the anniversary of her death. He spoke also of his uncle and aunt who had died in the *pika*, about his mother's hair falling out, and about his younger brother and sister: "The two little kids, three and five, they just vanished. Mother was in the house, and it fell in on her. She dug her way out but

77

she couldn't find a trace of them, nothing. They were there and then they were gone. They are 'whereabouts unknown,' even to today." He told me of the *pika* as he saw it (in one of the school work details 1,800 meters from the center), of the flash, and throwing himself down, and the great darkness that followed, and that only four or five of his group of about a hundred were alive when he looked up. And how, in agony with burns and blisters, he made his way with a teacher to a place near the water front, where ten days later his father found him.

And finally, idly wiping the bar with a damp cloth, stacking the cardboard coasters, he spoke of his failure to marry. "Those who have died are finished, forgotten. But what about people like me who are still living and cannot find happiness? This is what I want Americans to think about."

More than half a dozen times, Nakai-san has gone forth, expectant and tingling, to a *miai*, the formal meeting of prospective bride and groom that is part of the Japanese ritual of an arranged marriage. "But when the other parents saw me, they would call it off, and I would get word that they felt that if I got sick and died their daughter would become a widow, and that they were just trying to protect their daughter from that possibility, and I should try to understand

. . . But look at me. I'm healthy and strong, and running my own business, and I'm not so very ugly to look at in spite of these scars."

Even several potential love matches were broken up "when the parents and grandparents started putting the pressure on. There was one . . . I thought she was really cute, and I think she . . . Well, anyway, the family stopped it. Now I'm thirty-three, and I don't have much chance any more. The time for marriage is slipping by and I'm not hunting any more. To get slapped down like that all the time, it can change your attitude to life, can make you start feeling sorry for yourself, and I would rather not get into that kind of thinking. I'm glad to be alive. To have died would have been useless . . . Those girls? Now they're all married. If they're happy, that's fine. I want them to be happy. I'm just waiting for the one who will have a more understanding heart, and who won't be afraid of these . . . this face . . . How about another beer?"

No one knows how many scarred survivors of the Bomb live their lives in utter seclusion, afraid to be seen by any but their immediate families. A few who have to work and are otherwise healthy still go around with their heads swathed in white bandage, just to hide the ugly keloids. Two of the twenty-five scarred "Hiroshima Maidens" who were taken to New York for plastic surgery in 1954 have died; the rest are quietly leading fairly normal, healthy lives, and some have married and borne children. Other young women marked by the Bomb have learned to live with their condition, although in most cases it took a long time.

Tamae Nakatani, a Hiroshima primary schoolteacher, is one. Plump, neat and kindly, she wears lipstick and rakish harlequin spectacles that tag her as a lively, alert and outgoing woman. Only from up close can you notice that beneath the glasses her complexion is rough and darkened, as if she were suffering from a serious rash.

The Bomb caught Miss Nakatani and her classmates just a mile from the hypocenter, at work on the firebreaks. Three hundred out of 350 were killed outright. "Three or four of us," she states simply, "all badly burned and in tatters, tried to make our way across Hijiyama Bridge. As we went, blisters broke out on our skin, and the skin just seemed to slip right off our hands. Our legs were burned too and none of us could walk alone, but we all leaned on each other and somehow we managed to cross the river. There was an army depot there, so crowded with other people like us that we could only stand side-ways, as they say . . . And on the evening of the second day my father found me and took me home." She was thirteen.

Tamae's frantic parents twice carried her to one of the few shattered hospitals that were functioning. "I was pretty badly burned, but there were those who were even more terribly injured, and they had priority, so we went home. And of course, there were no medicines, so what we got to clean the wounds—it's embarrassing to speak of it—was the salty liquid from *umeboshi,* pickled plums, which is a pretty strong disinfectant. And for the burns we used cooking oil, what you use for *tempura,* and talcum, and mixed all these up and applied it. And when we looked for doctors, those few who had not been drafted by the army anyway, well, many had died. It was a sad time."

For the remainder of the year she stayed in bed. She could not stand; her legs were paralyzed. She could not move her right hand. "My mother massaged it for me every day, so now, you see, it's nearly normal." Later, "when I could go out again, I was frightened and would try to hide in doorways whenever I heard the sound of a plane. And I was terribly frightened of the Occupation soldiers and jeeps that were in the city. Not a question of whether they were bad or good—I was just scared of them."

By the following February makeshift schools had somehow reopened on the fringes of the devastated area, and Tamae, weak, disfigured and frightened, went back to class—"or I wouldn't have been promoted." Eventually, she graduated, became a teacher, and slowly began to regain the confidence that had been destroyed on an August morning. Slowly, too, she began to comprehend just what she could expect and what she could never demand from her life as a scarred *hibak'sha,* and started to accept it. At any rate, she stopped hiding.

"For ten years after the war I was afraid to live like everyone else. Even in the heat of summer I wore long sleeves like this, because as a young girl I did not want to show such ugly arms to others. But that was a grave mistake, psychologically and spiritually, and it made my parents and family terribly unhappy, because they could see from that what was in my mind. But then, instead of constantly telling myself that I was going to live a miserable and pitiable life, I had a sort of spiritual revolution within myself, and I decided not to think about my atomic scars. So on the tenth anniversary of the Bomb, I put on a short-sleeved dress for the first time and went to the memorial service. And ever since, like anyone else, I dress according to the weather."

But it is Hiroshima's hidden, invisible scars that can be most deadly. Toshio Kihara did not have a mark on him. He was a photoengraver's assistant, youthful, energetic, serious about learning his trade and enthusiastic about having his fun. He liked to fish in the Ota, and listen to jazz records until late at night, and up until the summer of 1964 he might have been found, from time to time, among the dance-hall *samurai* at the Casino. To watch him, no one would have known that his parents had both died in the Bomb, when he was four, and that he himself had spent a year and a half in the Atom Bomb Hospital when he was nineteen.

Toshio's illness was leukemia, but the doctors at the hospital insist that the boy himself had never been told. His married elder sister, with whom he lived, seems to have known. At any rate, in the spring of 1964 Toshio came home in high spirits one evening and announced to his sister and brother-in-law that he had found a girl and was going to get married. The families met each other, all was agreed, and a marriage was planned for the following spring. Toshio's sister couldn't bring herself to tell Toshio's fiancée, Matsue, about the leukemia. She assumed that the girl and her family would have heard of it through the usual thorough investigation of a marriage partner that all Japanese families undertake automatically. "And they were so happy, and he seemed so well. I didn't want to take the chance of spoiling anything."

Then, in September of 1964, Toshio Kihara fell sick again and re-entered the Atom Bomb Hospital. Matsue visited him frequently, and cheered him, and they continued to plan and dream together. But on December 5th of that year he died of acute leukemia, aged twenty-three. His sister and her husband say they were shocked as well as grieved, because they had had no hint that he was so ill. What Matsue felt can only be imagined now, because exactly seven days later she took an overdose of sleeping medicine and followed after her lover. Side by side their ashes rest; one stone serves them both, and on it is engraved: Toshio Kihara; Matsue, his wife.

Dr. Shigeto knew Kihara well, and spoke often to Matsue when she came to visit him. He is sure the boy did not know he had leukemia, "or he never would have become engaged." The doctor has so often seen the young struck down, and he knows that he carries an invisible scar himself. Yet he is able to maintain composure, and reason, and moderation. "What happened in wartime could not be helped," he says. "Together Japan and America have dispelled the hatred. You haven't found hatred or bitterness in Hiroshima, have you?" he asked me.

Yes, Doctor, I have. It runs in a narrow stream, but deep, and only among those who have never been able to stand again. I don't find it elsewhere in Japan, and it refuses to be diverted by cool reason or warm kindness. Not everyone in the world is like you, Dr. Shigeto, and maybe that's why we have wars.

In a darkened parlor, a shabby Western-style room, they are waiting for me to come to hear them, three middle-aged and elderly *hibak'sha,* steeped in venom. Michiyoshi Nukushina, fifty-eight, lost his left leg in the Bomb; Ikujiro Tanekyo, seventy, lost all his relatives and children and thus, vitally important to a Japanese, his chance for immortality and the right to support in his old age; Mrs. Mine Ebisudani, seventy, lost her health and the little wealth she had. All are ill, out-patients at the A-Bomb Hospital. "It would take us until tomorrow morning to explain our bitterness," says Nukushina, who has been told by a mutual friend only that I would like them to speak to me frankly. "Please ask us anything."

His voice is sharp and biting, his eyes flash, and he knocks on his wooden leg to emphasize his points and to remind his listeners of his credentials. He has only four months to live, but neither he nor his listeners are aware of it. "Look what America has done to us! The Bomb violated international law; a Japanese court decided that just recently. This old man here will never have grandchildren. There are *hibak'-sha* who can't get the medical attention they need because they can't afford to stop working to go into the hospital. They die unattended, with no doctor even to make it easier . . ." The other two are nodding, murmuring assent. In the background, Nukushina's wife, a tiny sparrow of a woman who runs their grocery shop, tries to blunt his attack, but he waves her off. He has found an audience and is warming up.

"Why did America drop such a terrible weapon when Japan was losing the war and was going to surrender anyway? Racial discrimination, that's why. I heard that the Bomb was produced two years before it was used, so why wasn't it used against Germany? Why, eh? Why?"

I start to protest, to explain the history, to point out that if the Bomb had been ready earlier, it would have been used on Japan much sooner. But Nukushina is laughing, almost sneering, and rapping on his leg, and I desist, for there is no seat for logic in this stuffy room.

Mrs. Ebisudani, eyes wide in her long, sad face, is talking with the simple childlike assurance of the very old. "Didn't they drop it for an experiment? Weren't they just making guinea pigs of us? When I went to the A.B.C.C. they took blood from me, even though they promised they wouldn't. They took five cc.'s and I fainted and I've been sicker since then, but I don't go back, I don't trust them there . . . My son and his wife are both *hibak'sha* and I worry about my grandson, who is in the fifth grade now, and weakly. I worry about whether this innocent boy, who knows nothing about the Bomb, will be affected by the dreadful sickness too. The doctors tell me to eat meat and nourishing food, but if we buy good food we have nothing left for clothes at all. How can my husband and I live on our eight thousand yen [twenty-three dollars] a month?"

Tanekyo, the man who has not even sickly grandchildren, wears dark glasses and a tight, cruel grin, and he punctuates his sentences with gruff chuckles, as if deriving some bitter and final revenge from telling off an American at last. "Japan would never have dropped such a weapon if we had developed it.

In prewar Japan we honored *bushido,* the code of the *samurai,* which protects women and children instead of slaughtering them. It is the civilians like us in Hiroshima who are the most wretched, because we have suffered in the Bomb but do not get the pensions and other aid that soldiers receive."

"It is unavoidable if soldiers are killed in a war," says Mrs. Ebisudani, "but I get terribly angry when I think how many civilians like me were hurt in Hiroshima."

"The *ayamachi,*" says Nukushina, "the error, was not Japan's. It means those who dropped the Bomb were at fault. That's what Nehru said when he came here. He made it very clear."

"Maybe you think it means war itself," says Tanekyo with one of his ghastly laughs, "but those who died in the Bomb were not the ones who made war."

"The world just doesn't understand the terror of the A-Bomb as we do," says Nukushina, "and it doesn't realize how the effects of it go on and on . . . And if, as you argue, the Bomb was dropped to save lives and end the war quickly, then it should not have been dropped on us here in Hiroshima, but it should have been dropped on Tokyo instead."

The martyrs of Hiroshima may be many, but the saints are few.

4°

It is the helpless who nourish their hate; it is those so thoroughly mauled by the Bomb that they have never reaped any of the pleasures of postwar Japan who can discuss the event only in snarls and shouts, devoid of reason. "War turns humans into animals," old Tanekyo said at one point, and he could have added that peace does not always reverse the process. But those *hibak'sha* who have achieved a reasonable standard of life, who can support themselves, are beginning to feel that acts of war cannot be weighed on normal scales—and that is why they shout for peace. Even the scarred among them acknowledge quietly that if Japan had developed the Bomb first, she would have dropped it, the code of *bushido* notwithstanding. Hiroshima, over all, is reluctant to hate, but it is clear that no new golden qualities of the human spirit emerged from the crucible of the atomic blast. Given the choice, the majority would probably have agreed with Nukushina that the Bomb should have been dropped on Tokyo.

Mrs. Barbara Reynolds, an American Quaker and pacifist, has lived for years in Hiroshima, helping the survivors tell their story to the world, but she is not blind to their faults. "Among the survivors of Hiroshima and Nagasaki," she says, "I have wonderful friends, but I have not felt that their deep desire for a world without war has made them more peaceful, more tolerant, more loving and kind than any of the rest of us." It would be surprising, of course, if it had.

"The most terrible thing about the Bomb was its destruction of the human heart. In an earthquake, or a normal bombing, everyone tries to help everyone else. But when you have been Atom-Bombed, that impulse vanishes." The speaker is Ichiro Kawamoto, a scrawny scarecrow of a man, with big ears, rotting teeth and melancholy eyes, who years ago resigned himself to a life of impoverished misery and quietly dedicated it to helping victims worse off than he. "Perhaps it's meddling to do kindnesses for people, but I think it's better for society to do them than not to do them." A tattered apparition in scuffed sneakers and shabby coat, Kawamoto is welcome in hundreds of *hibak'sha* homes, especially in the poorest houses and those where illness lives, and he knows what these most unfortunate of the *hibak'sha* are thinking. Now, as he led me through the dusty ramshackle streets of the Fukushima-cho district, where thousands of the poorest *hibak'sha* live, he was trying to explain the psychological effect of the Bomb, and how it differed from conventional war.

"The destruction is too sudden, too complete for anyone to think of others. You try to escape yourself, and there is no escape; you try to find water or food, but there is none; and even if there are people worse off than you are, you just don't care, you don't have the heart or the strength to care about anyone but yourself and your family . . . And those who are suffering, no matter how much they shout to passers-by for help, no one responds, and so they lose faith in people. And you lose faith in yourself too. Even when we wanted to help, we didn't know what to do, where to start. I even thought at one point that I should have killed some of them to put them out of their misery."

Without warning, without escape or succor, the entire known world of familiar houses where recognizable individuals lived, and of friends who bowed in the street when you passed, and water that came out of taps, and doctors with medicines to treat you if you were ill—suddenly the entire edifice collapsed. Buddhists thought they had gone to Hell—not that it was *like* Hell, but that they were really there. According to Yoko Ohta, a poet, Hiroshima in the days soon after the Bomb did not look like a city destroyed by war but like "a fragment of a world that was ending."

In *Records of the Hiroshima Experience,* an anthology of personal narratives banned by the Occupation and published finally in 1965, a man named Katsumi Kojima, who was a student at the time of the Bomb, described the moments after the explosion and then wrote: ". . . I ran to the shelter. The only thing I considered all this time was how to save myself . . . We came to the Red Cross Hospital but the road was filled with the debris of houses, and refugees were attempting to walk through this crowded street. Here and there, bloody victims who could not even move were lying on the ground. Those who could move stepped on these obstacles and kept on in order to save their own lives. I saw the selfishness of human nature. Since we could not get through the street, we entered the hospital . . . Nurses were trying desperately to save those who were buried under debris. My friend suggested we help, but I replied, 'Don't be foolish, you yourself are wounded. Let's go to my room' . . . I do not have courage to describe my heartless conduct after this. With my friend I escaped to Hijiyama . . . The sight and sound of the desperate pleas of the dying I cannot forget. I cannot recall that day without a strong sense of guilt, and I feel that I did something terrible."

There may be little difference morally between the Atom Bomb and the "conventional" saturation bombings of Rotterdam, London, Stuttgart, Tokyo and other cities in World War II—they all killed large numbers of noncombatants. But those who lived through Hiroshima insist that for the victims, there is no comparison. Even in the March 9, 1945, incendiary raid on Tokyo, which killed 76,056 people, they point out, thousands of uninjured persons remained to help the hurt, facilities of some sort were maintained to shelter them, there had been some warning, and some way to flee, and time to hide—at least for the majority. But in Hiroshima, one out of every three or four persons was killed immediately or fatally stricken, and the others were hurt too badly and were too dazed to be of any help to each other. Entire households were wiped out in the instant of the *pika*, or, what was worse, the only survivor of a family was sometimes one small panicky child struggling in tears through the rubble to where he thought his home had been, to find nothing, and no one.

Seared by their doomsday experience, even those survivors who have put hate aside remain unappeased by what came later. Seichi Ariya is another conservative Hondori shopkeeper, a friend and neighbor of Sera the furniture dealer, and he is grateful for postwar American aid to Japan. But, he says, "I will never be satisfied with the fact that the man who dropped the Bomb on Hiroshima, wiping out more than a hundred thousand noncombatants, became a hero and was decorated, while Japanese military leaders were executed for carrying out similar awful deeds of war. There is a terrible injustice there. If one was an atrocity, so was the other; if one was justified, and worthy of a medal, then they all were. A fair country like America should be able to distinguish between right and wrong."

"Lots of people come to Hiroshima and Nagasaki today, looking for a different mood, to discover something new in the minds or the spirits of the people here," says Kawamoto. "But what they discover is that workers are working hard, and the students are studying hard, and everyone is looking out for himself. Where is the feeling of peace? Only on the sign-post of the inn and in the souvenir cookies do you find the feeling of peace. It's like when you go to Kyoto or Nara, you learn of the history that must not be forgotten but it's no longer part of the lives of the people there."

In a small, sad way, Kawamoto and his perky wife Tokie are attempting to keep the feeling alive among some of the people of Hiroshima. Their tiny house is headquarters for the *Orizuru No Kai,* the Paper Crane Society, which they founded and advise. Folding paper cranes, Japan's traditional "get well" symbol, is only a minor activity of the eighty or so junior high school and high school students who belong to the *Kai.* Most of the time the members are crisscrossing the city on errands of assistance for the *hibak'sha,* washing clothes for those who don't have the energy, cooking for others, baby-sitting for mothers who have to get hospital checkups, and visiting hospitals themselves to cheer patients with garlands of paper cranes and other small gifts. They organize parties to raise money, which is distributed by the Kawamotos to the *hibak'sha* in greatest need, place death notices in the newspapers when Bomb victims with no families die, and sometimes are the only people to attend the funeral of a survivor. It's grim and morbid work for teen-aged schoolgirls—but Tokie Kawamoto herself was just thirteen when she saw and smelled and felt the horrors of the Bomb, and it doesn't occur to her or to anyone else in Hiroshima that a preoccupation with disease and death is not the healthiest frame of mind for a growing girl.

For other reasons entirely, the *Kai* is ignored or ridiculed by many Japanese. Its activities are outside the Japanese pattern: it is helping people to whom no favor is owed, and from whom no favor can be expected in return.

Yoko Akimoto, a sixteen-year-old high school girl, is one of the ten members who do most of the work of the *Kai;* she realizes why the majority of Hiroshima's students are just not interested. "People who live outside of Hiroshima seem more interested in this kind of organization, in the Atom Bomb, and in peace. It seems that students in Hiroshima, and adults too, try to run away from any thought of the Bomb, or of radiation sickness, for they are always facing it, their lives are surrounded by it every day. They don't want to think about it more than they have to. But people outside of Hiroshima, those who have not been affected, they can think about it more easily, without a burden of sadness . . . We get lots of requests from people in other cities who want to join,

96

but we have to limit it to those within the city, and we can't get enough."

"There are lots of people who *say* that they are willing to help the work of the society, but somehow they hesitate to become members," says Kazuhiro Sasaki, the only university student in the *Kai*. "They say they are too shy to join, for if they are members they have to take some kind of initiative, and they don't want to attract attention. For instance, we wear our *Kai* armbands when we visit *hibak'sha* homes, and some feel embarrassed about that . . . But when I think of the *hibak'sha*, I am not embarrassed. There is no organization which really helps them, and they get fishy looks from other people when they go out to do the chores that we do for them now . . . So we are not embarrassed. We are proud to be members of this organization."

Great clusters of paper cranes hang over the leukemia victims' hospital beds. Smiles of welcome and sometimes tears of relief greet the *Kai* members on their rounds. For *hibak'sha* too old, too weak to manage alone, the services of the *Kai* are often indispensable. But the others don't want the pity or the extra help. They are getting along somehow, and they don't want to stand out from the mainstream of Japanese life.

The entire Japanese nation, however, bears the traumatic scar of the nuclear experience. Even as they turn their eyes from the suffering of individual *hibak'sha,* and murmur that Hiroshima is selling its scars for tourism or for politics, many Japanese coddle the notion that the Bomb fell on all of them. What happens to individuals in Hiroshima may not concern the man in Tokyo or Osaka, but what happens to "our country" matters deeply. The fact that Japan was the only nation to see the *pika* is a consideration never far from his consciousness when he reads a newspaper account of war anywhere, or squats down before his television set to be lectured at by the many "men of culture" who tell him precisely what the news may mean, and who never let him forget Japan's unique place in history.

There is no doubt that the experience of the Bomb has deepened the pacifist sentiments of postwar Japan. Ichiro Iwatate, the wise editor-in-chief of Kyodo, Japan's principal news service, explains that "Hiroshima is our symbol of war. Whenever we hear of any kind of war, we immediately see that mushroom cloud. Every time there is a nuclear test anywhere, newspaper editors scream for pictures of the cloud. It is the key to Japanese pacifism. I'm sure that the memory of war, the abhorrence of war, would have faded much sooner without that symbol. And I think it will remain the same for another ten or twenty years. Japanese, who are terrified of nuclear war, immediately fear that any small war anywhere will lead to atomic bombing, and that's one reason for the Japanese attitude to Vietnam . . . One result of this anti-war sentiment, of course, is that the government doesn't dare spend much money for national defense, and this has helped our economic recovery."

Japan's worship of peace underlies the thinking even of conservatives like Sera and his son, the furniture dealers on the Hondori. They are annoyed by the way August 6th has become "an occasion for waving red flags in Hiroshima," but, said the elder Sera, "we are in favor of a non-political peace movement."

And what might that be?

"We want to prohibit all nuclear wars, and outlaw nuclear weapons entirely, for all time."

But surely, in today's world, I ventured, that is a political position.

"No, that's not political. Everybody here feels that way. Whatever happens, the tragedies of Hiroshima and Nagasaki must not be repeated."

The fact that Japan has tasted the ultimate horror

of war is of course only one of the reasons why Japanese devotion to the ideal of peace approaches the blind faith which in earlier days was directed toward the Emperor and war. An equally impelling reason is Japan's dependence on trade. Lacking domestic supplies of raw materials for her industries, and having discovered that military conquest is not the way to get them, even conservative Japanese business leaders believe that war, cutting off shipping and drying up sources of material, would mean disaster for Japan. Large continental nations like the United States, the Soviet Union and China might be able to pick up the pieces and start over again after a nuclear conflict, but if Japan were involved, the 98,000,-000 Japanese in this tiny land would surely perish.

Japan's defeat, the first in her history, laid bare the guts of the nation. Cowering in shock, the Japanese avidly tried to soak up everything the victor murmured. Not all the reforms of the Occupation could penetrate, but the idealism of the immediate postwar period did. Peace, democracy, freedom, neutrality—these were the ideals reflected in the new constitution drafted in General MacArthur's headquarters, and even today some Japanese still daydream of Japan's becoming the Switzerland of the Orient. One of the key clauses in the constitution is

the famous Article Nine, which renounces war forever as an instrument of government policy. After
Hiroshima, the Japanese were only too happy to accept the idea. Nowadays the United States government would like to see the clause eliminated, while
the "anti-imperialist" left is struggling hardest to
keep this American brainstorm in Japan's constitution.

The leaders of this large, vocal and well-organized
Japanese left—now commanding the loyalty of about
forty percent of the electorate—think that America
dropped the A-Bomb primarily to contain Soviet
Russia's postwar sphere of influence. A few United
States historians recently have speculated that one
reason the Bomb was used without thoroughly prob-
ing Japan's attitude toward surrender—specifically,
without offering Japan the assurance the Emperor
would not be deposed—was to block Soviet power.
The United States, this theory goes, believed that the
promised Soviet attack on Japan could, even without
the Bomb, push the tottering, beaten nation of Japan
into final and immediate collapse, leaving Stalin with
a stronger hand in postwar diplomacy.

Whatever the motives of the leaders in Washington, it is clear in retrospect that the Bomb effectively
stymied the Soviets. According to President Truman

himself, "Our dropping of the atomic bomb . . . forced Russia to reconsider her position in the Far East." America, having demonstrated its atomic power, no longer needed to make concessions; it was Moscow that yielded, on China and other questions. The Russians were compelled to drop their demands for a role in the occupation of Japan, and Japan was spared a tragic division such as Germany's.

Thoughtful Japanese realize now what happened. "Many of us are grateful for the U.S. occupation," says Kenzo Suzuki, a former foreign correspondent on the staff of the *Asahi Shimbun*. "We are glad the Russians did not come in and occupy us, and despite the horrors and suffering caused by the Bomb, we recognize the strategic importance of Hiroshima in this respect."

Remaining united geographically, Japan was nonetheless divided ideologically, and the left early took the lead in the campaign against the weapon that had made capitalist America predominant. And even faster than in other countries, the word *peace* became an ideological and emotional term, because the Japanese were already obsessed with it.

The "Peace Movement" itself began as an idealistic and non-political housewives' petition in 1954, after Japanese fishermen ran into fallout from the Bikini

H-Bomb test. In August of the following year, the tenth anniversary of Hiroshima, the first international Ban-the-Bomb meeting took place there, and out of that conference grew the organization known as "Gensuikyo," which is a shortened form of the name for the Japan Council for the Prohibition of Atomic and Hydrogen Bombs. And by 1960 Gensuikyo was deeply involved in demonstrations against the U.S.-Japan Security Treaty, and simultaneously demanding Red China's admission to the U.N.

Ichiro Kawamoto blames official indifference for the almost obscene speed with which the left captured the movement. There has never been an opportunity, he points out, for ordinary citizens to attend any of the memorial services or rallies. Schools, factories and offices remain open on August 6th, for example, and the only people who can attend are officials whose jobs are connected with the event, and representatives of unions or student organizations, usually leftist-controlled, who have authorized time off. "There should be a way for those without ideology to attend," he insists.

Instead, the Peace Movement became a battleground for ideology. The first clash came in 1961, when Gensuikyo condemned American nuclear tests but said nothing about those of the Soviet Union.

Two rival organizations were formed that year, and even the Japan Socialist Party delegates walked out of a Tokyo meeting in 1962 because the Communists controlling Gensuikyo refused to send nuclear test protest telegrams to Moscow as well as to Washington.

The next year the Soviet delegation walked out of the international meeting when Peking-line delegates, aligned with the Japan Communist Party, forced through a resolution condemning the U.S.– Soviet Partial Test Ban Treaty. But in Hiroshima, a few days later, it was the Peking group that bolted, because everyone else supported the treaty. That sent ultra-leftist students of the Zengakuren into a rowdy, riotous demonstration around the cenotaph in the green and hallowed Park of Peace.

When the dust cleared from that chilling spectacle, Hiroshima, and most of Japan, had awakened; and conscientious pacifists like Barbara Reynolds, who had invested time and money in helping Hiroshima make its "appeal," and had innocently been used by the left, were learning, as she put it, "that the problems of the world are more complicated than had appeared at first sight."

By 1964, when the Chinese Communists began nuclear testing, the split was deep. But those who hoped the Chinese bomb would silence the Communists in Japan were wrong. The Japan Communist Party, which subscribes to the Peking line, defied the feelings of the *hibak'sha* and supported the Chinese "right to defend themselves from American aggression." Gensuikyo, incredibly, went along, and the mask had vanished.

Consequently, five separate sets of memorial services and rallies marked the twentieth anniversary of the Bomb in 1965. On the morning of August 6th, 30,000 citizens of Hiroshima, most of them *hibak'sha,* gathered at the Park of Peace for the city's official service, while millions of Japanese watched on television throughout Japan. Dark, scudding rain clouds —the edge of a typhoon—raced low over the city, bringing splashes of large warm drops, and some of the people in the crowd couldn't help thinking of what their lives would have held if the weather had been like that twenty years before. At exactly 8:15, two twenty-year-old youths, representing the victims' families, swung the great beam to ring the Peace Bell; temple gongs and church bells picked up the message and the wail of a siren echoed across the motionless city. All cars and streetcars and buses came to a halt; factory and office workers on their way to work stopped in their tracks; in the Peace

Park crowd there were sobs, and tears, and the slight shuffle of feet on gravel. The voice of a small child, too young to understand, but quickly hushed, carried far, and the typhoon gusts cuffed at the eternal flame, and whispered through paper cranes on the Children's Monument, and riffled the surface of the river below the Dome.

Later, a thousand doves were released, and wreaths were laid at the cenotaph, and officials clapped their hands softly together, bowed their heads, and murmured quiet Buddhist prayers for the dead. Mayor Hamai placed a plaque with 469 new names—including that of Toshio Kihara—in the granite receptacle under the cenotaph. A long line formed, and for hours, despite the rain and wind, the citizens of Hiroshima filed up to the cenotaph in family groups, by twos and threes—and singly—to pray, to commune briefly with the departed, and to remember.

A few hours later the Hiroshima Survivors Association, a conservative group led by the local city political bosses, held its own memorial service. That was followed in the afternoon by Gensuikyo's eleventh World Conference, which had earlier heard a message from Indonesia's President Sukarno declaring that "nuclear weapons in the hands of the new emerging forces are weapons for the defense of peace and independence, while nuclear weapons in the hands of the imperialists become the tools of war and colonization."

At the same time the Socialists and SOHYO were rallying elsewhere in Hiroshima. Their new organization, the Japan *Congress* Against Atomic and Hydrogen Weapons, is opposed to all nations' nuclear weapons, but it skirted cautiously around the issue of the Chinese tests and emphasized Vietnam. Socialist Party Secretary General Tomomi Narita told the group that "we intend to make strong demands that the U.S. withdraw from Vietnam and we will fight the Sato government, which is assisting America's aggressive policy."

Finally, the smallest and quietest of the anti-Bomb rallies were those sponsored by a vaguely liberal group of intellectuals and the moderate Democratic Socialist Party. The National Congress Against Nuclear Arms and for World Peace protests nuclear weaponry of all nations, and says no more. Which of course is what most Hiroshima *hibak'sha* approve of —except for the fact that this group is sponsored by a political party, and thus political, and now taboo. Hiroshima residents tend to laugh grimly at this group because it installed in the Peace Park the "eternal flame," with an inscription that it shall burn

until all nuclear weapons everywhere are dismantled
—but then it failed to provide enough money to keep
the gas jet going twenty-four hours a day, so the
"eternal" flame is turned off most nights along about
midnight.

"Japan," ran an editorial in the *Yomiuri Shimbun*
at about the time of the anniversary, "has an inesca-
pable duty to struggle against forces which might
unleash nuclear warfare upon humanity. This twentieth anniversary year of the atomic explosions over
Hiroshima and Nagasaki is a focal moment to sum-
mon all mankind to the banner of peace. But peace
cannot be a plaything of political ideologies. Why
then are we faced in Japan with ideological warfare
at a time when the sufferings of the 1945 nuclear
bombing victims should be our solemn reminder of
a duty to see that such tragedies never happen
again?"

The answer, the *Yomiuri* said, is that "the original
high purpose has been lost . . . and subverted";
Hiroshima's dead, and "the great crusade against
nuclear warfare," have been "betrayed."

"What other country but Japan can drive home the
limitless suffering [nuclear] weapons inflict?" the
Yomiuri asked. And what other Japanese but the *hibak'sha*? Yoko Akimoto, of the Paper Crane Society,

said: "We feel it is the duty of those of us who are living here to help the *hibak'sha* as best we can, and to tell the story of Hiroshima to the world."

The Dome is one voice telling the story. Iwatate, the Kyodo editor, is concerned that the Communists and leftists will exploit the Dome, but thinks it should be kept nevertheless, "as a reminder of what the A-Bomb can do." But the president of the Toyo Kogyo auto company, Tsuneji Matsuda, wonders if the Dome won't have an effect contrary to what is intended by letting it stand. "The atom bombs of the future," he points out, "won't leave anything around that looks like that. They would wreak even greater havoc, and to leave the Dome there will make future generations think that the Bomb is not so terrible after all."

This concern for future generations is a crucial part of the thinking of all the people of Hiroshima. Mayor Hamai, a wise politician, has managed to avoid a decision on the Dome by suggesting it be left as it is "until the next generation decides what to do with it." Hamai understands the desire of his fellow citizens to leave a proper legacy, and also their feelings today. Without the Dome, Hiroshima would have only the pain and the fading memory. And without the public scar on the bank of the Ota, the private pains would be that much harder to bear. But, for many, there are considerations deeper than symbolism.

I spoke one evening to a cheery, pink-faced butcher in Fukushima-cho, one of the poorest sections of the city. Like most of his neighbors, he is a member of Japan's old outcast class, the *burakumin,* and that is why I will just call him Mr. M. Despite legal equality the *burakumin* still face discrimination in jobs, marriage and housing throughout Japan, and this permanent, unchanging burden they all carry weighs more heavily on their lives than the discrimination against *hibak'sha* in general. Although Mr. M. is a fairly prosperous tradesman by *buraku* standards (there are *two* television sets in his home), his butcher's trade is one of those "unclean" jobs traditionally left to the outcasts to perform (because of the Buddhist prohibition against killing animals), and he lives with his family in what can only be described as a slum.

Mr. M. himself did not see the Bomb that destroyed his city. He was a private in the army and returned home later. His wife and eldest children, however, were two kilometers from the hypocenter, had their house collapse on them, and later walked through the black radioactive rain that fell on their part of the city. So far, they are all healthy, and their son has been married—"to the daughter of another butcher," that is, within their class.

Poorly educated, still an outcast, his new prosperity hard-won, Butcher M. nevertheless is concerned with the human spirit. Perhaps this concern springs from a lifetime of discrimination. The Dome, he fears, "may make the younger generation too servile. They can read about the Bomb in books. They don't need this fearsome monument to frighten them. It's true it will make them hate war, but it will prevent them from developing a broader mind. It doesn't really bother me, but it's not good to feel penitent all the time. If we keep it, it continues the sadness in the Japanese mind. Children who know nothing about it will always be reminded that an American plane came during the war and dropped the *pikadon* —innocent children who had no connection with it— and these children will be used by politicians to affect the future co-operation between the United States and Japan."

The children of Hiroshima early become aware of the fact that their city, and some of their parents, are special. But the gap between what they learn and the experiences of those who teach them is already more than wide enough to explain why young Nishi-ura, who wants to learn jazz, is a true representative of his generation.

Tamae Nakatani, the scarred girl who wore long sleeves for ten years, entered the teaching profession just because of the Bomb. Having been exposed to heavy radiation just 1.5 kilometers from the hypo-center, she was advised never to exert herself physi-cally. So instead of joining her brothers and sisters in the family oyster business ("we produce the best oysters in all of Hiroshima"), she went on to junior college and became a teacher. "I think it was very fortunate that I went into teaching. If you put your heart into that work, for a woman, well . . ." She paused, thoughtful. "You can see the children grow-ing before your eyes . . . I don't think you can find that kind of happiness in other kinds of work. It's good to be a teacher." Especially, she seemed to be saying, for a woman who will probably never have children of her own.

Tamae started teaching primary school at the age of twenty, in the same school district where she had "met the *pika*" seven years before. Undoubtedly the teaching job, her ability to cope with it, and the na-tural exuberance of the children helped her find the courage she needed to bare her unsightly arms. But the courage must have been there.

There are not many teachers in the world who have emerged whole and sane from this kind of psychological meat grinder; a child could learn a lot from Tamae Nakatani, and she has taught hundreds by now, in all the lower grades. "When I tell them that I, their teacher, have gone through this experience, the children in my class are extremely serious, and they pay strict attention. Once, in the schoolyard, I heard some children behind me laughing at the scars on my legs. I turned around to them and quietly explained that I was burned in the Atom Bomb and that I am lucky to be alive because only twenty in my class of three hundred and fifty girls are still living, and they listened very seriously and walked away slowly, quite thoughtful."

Third-grade pupils in Hiroshima schools study the history of their city. "As part of that curriculum," says Nakatani-*sensei,* "one unit about the Bomb is always included, as part of the story of how Hiroshima developed, and to compare Hiroshima of past and present. We don't say much about the causes of the war, just that it happened, and that Japan's allies were defeated in Europe, and the United States and

Britain were chasing us down, and that the people of that time had nothing to eat and nothing to wear. And we tell them that the Bomb was dropped, and all the houses were burned. We show them pictures of that time, and we teach about the grief and pain, and how so many people, a hundred and fifty thousand, were killed. And then, how everyone co-operated until we have built up this fine city that they see today. We don't touch the moral issue. We don't give them anything about whether the Bomb was justified or not. We have to take a neutral attitude, and we are forbidden to make any value judgments or take any biased positions. We just emphasize that war is a fearful thing, in which, in Hiroshima's case, so many tens of thousands of people were killed. So from the actual facts of Hiroshima the children can appreciate clearly the horror and fearfulness of war."

Miss Nakatani's own views, which she cannot teach, parallel the opinions of many *hibak'sha* who have found a niche and some comfort in the Atomic Age. "Maybe it's just that I'm getting older and more tolerant, but I'm not afraid of Americans any more, especially since such a wonderful person as President Kennedy appeared there. And I realize that America probably was forced into the war . . . And if the Bomb had not been dropped, perhaps the war would have lasted much longer. We may have fought from village to village. That's our national character, you know, to fight to the end, even though there were some people who advised the government to stop even before the Bomb fell. And from the point of view of humanity in general, the fact that so many people were killed in an instant might have been a good lesson, that war is a fearful thing. So in a way, although it's terrible to say this because it was such a terrible tragedy"—and her voice dropped almost to a whisper—"maybe it has contributed something to the world."

Her eyes were moist behind the sporty spectacles. "Anyway," she said, passing her plump hand lightly over her face, "the Bomb is something finished, and even if I were to hate, that hate wouldn't make these marks of the Bomb go away, so there's no use blaming anybody. I only hope such a tragedy shall never be repeated."

Over and over, like a prayer, a ritual chant, a magic password, or like a lesson to be stamped indelibly on the minds of every child in every class in every year, Miss Nakatani had reiterated that phrase, the phrase on the cenotaph: ". . . [it] shall not be repeated," *kurikaesa-nai.* To the rest of the world, such a wish is so obvious that it seems trite to utter it.

But for the *hibak'sha* of Hiroshima, to whom nuclear warfare is not a nightmare but a fact of life, it cannot be overstated.

It is the automatic repetition of the phrase, and the emphasis on the evils of war rather than on the causes, that makes Japanese so quick to see the potential holocaust in every conflict anywhere. Aware of no threat to themselves in the policies of Communist China, or at least no threat more awful than that of the Bomb, the Japanese cannot understand United States policy in Vietnam. Americans in Japan, and especially in Hiroshima, are continually confronted with the demand to "get out of Vietnam." The United States, some students who surrounded me in the Park of Peace one afternoon insisted, should meet any Communist threat to Asia by helping to improve the area "instead of sending troops, which only gives the impression that the natives are being oppressed by foreigners." To many Japanese, the news of American planes bombing Asians in Vietnam automatically switched on the vision of Hiroshima and the mushroom cloud.

In the Bar Yodel, Manabu Nakai leans on the counter and muses about the Atomic Dome. He imagines it "as a signpost to guide future generations to the history of Japan, as the Roman Forum does for Rome." Down at the end of the tiny bar, a young couple are sipping beer and listening, and nodding their heads. The girl, bright and pretty and slickly groomed, was born just a few months before the Bomb; her mother was severely burned, and "five or six close relatives," including two grandparents, died. Now she says, "If the Dome goes, a hole will open in our hearts. Like Japan has Mt. Fuji, Hiroshima has the Dome. Hiroshima without the Dome would be an unutterable disappointment and sadness." She is staring at her glass, moody and sad in the soft amber light from behind the bar, and for a moment one of Nakai's yodel records, turned down soft, is the only sound. She wants to talk—this is her first conversation with an American—and her boy friend, silently smiling, acquiesces. But she shies abruptly away from political questions. "I never touch that kind of thing." At length I mention the inscription on the cenotaph and ask her what *"ayamachi"* refers to. Her answer is quick: *"Ayamachi* means that war was a mistake. We are Japanese, so we don't want to say that we are bad, but we cannot say that we were all without guilt."

Few in Japan will go much further than that in taking responsibility for the Pacific war, or for Pearl Harbor; there is not much of a sense of moral absolutes in Japan, anyway. The Japanese do, pragmatically, acknowledge that the war, and their part in starting it, was a mistake. It is fruitless—and frustrating—to try to remind Japanese of Pearl Harbor when they bring up the "error" of Hiroshima, for they have already in a sense apologized for their mistake, and their regret is real; they have taken their punishment, are paying reparations, and therefore feel absolved. But the other side has not been punished, and Sera the furniture man can say that now America "should acknowledge a spiritual responsibility at least. Americans should feel apologetic for what they have done to the people of Hiroshima."

The shadows fade; the dancing fountain sprays its silly folderol; sleek cars pop like gorgeous baubles from relentless production lines to roll and skitter down the wide and handsome streets; the Kanawa sits low in the water with its cargo of beer, and the records go 'round and 'round in the Hondori shops, and isn't this a fine and hustling city, says the cab driver to the airport passenger, and he is right. They are dying, sooner, in the hospital, and suffering, in silence, in the slums, and they are complaining in darkened rooms like Nukushina's, and they are remembering everywhere. But the dying of course will die, and the living memories will vanish. And what will finally remain, besides a name, and a museum, and a granite marker, and a vague uncertainty in future generations?

For one thing, a difference never to be bridged. The victors, unharmed and "unpunished" in the homeland, are willing to resort to arms in the defense of freedoms. But the Japanese, who know what nuclear doomsday would look like, will believe for a long, long time that war is the worst possible evil, that no price is too high to pay for the *pika* never to flash again.

ABOUT THE AUTHOR

RAFAEL STEINBERG's personal knowledge of the Orient began accumulating in 1951 when International News Service dispatched him to Korea as a war correspondent. The following year he joined the *Time* Tokyo bureau. A stint as a *Time* writer in New York came later, and after that, three years as a correspondent in London. He resigned from the magazine in 1958 to write a play (not yet produced).

The chance to return to Japan lured Mr. Steinberg back to journalism, and he became Far Eastern Correspondent/Tokyo Bureau Chief for *Newsweek* in 1959. His extensive reporting on Japan, his ability in the language, and his personal contacts on many levels of Japanese society have equipped him with a broad understanding of the land and its people.

Since resigning from *Newsweek* in 1963, Mr. Steinberg has written articles on Japan for the *Saturday Evening Post*, the *Washington Post*, *The Reporter*, and other publications.

He was born in Newark, New Jersey, in 1927, grew up in Manhattan, served in the Navy for a year, and graduated *cum laude* from Harvard in 1950. At present, he and his wife and two daughters are living in Tokyo.

0